BUSINESS ENGLISH CORRESPONDENCE
(2nd Edition)

商务英语函电
（第二版）

吴雯 吴含 编著

图书在版编目(CIP)数据

商务英语函电 / 吴雯，吴含编著. —2版. —北京：北京大学出版社，2023.9
21世纪英语专业系列教材
ISBN 978-7-301-34434-7

Ⅰ.①商… Ⅱ.①吴… ②吴… Ⅲ.①国际商务–英语–电报信函–写作 Ⅳ.① F740

中国国家版本馆 CIP 数据核字 (2023) 第 174719 号

书　　　名	商务英语函电（第二版）
	SHANGWU YINGYU HANDIAN (DI-ER BAN)
著作责任者	吴　雯　吴　含　编著
责 任 编 辑	初艳红
标 准 书 号	ISBN 978-7-301-34434-7
出 版 发 行	北京大学出版社
地　　　址	北京市海淀区成府路 205 号　100871
网　　　址	http://www.pup.cn　新浪微博：@ 北京大学出版社
电 子 邮 箱	编辑部 pupwaiwen@pup.cn　总编室 zpup@pup.cn
电　　　话	邮购部 010-62752015　发行部 010-62750672　编辑部 010-62759634
印 刷 者	河北滦县鑫华书刊印刷厂
经 销 者	新华书店
	787 毫米 ×1092 毫米　16 开本　15.25 印张　450 千字
	2023 年 9 月第 1 版　2023 年 9 月第 1 次印刷
定　　　价	49.00 元

未经许可，不得以任何方式复制或抄袭本书之部分或全部内容。
版权所有，侵权必究
举报电话：010-62752024　电子邮箱：fd@pup.cn
图书如有印装质量问题，请与出版部联系，电话：010-62756370

前　言

自从中国加入 WTO 后，随着全球经济的发展和市场化的运作，对商务人才的培养也提出了新的要求。优秀的商务人员不仅需要掌握国际上通行的贸易做法和商务程序，有一定的国际商务实际操作经验，而且要具备商务英语沟通能力和函电写作技巧，以适应充满机遇和挑战的时代，成为成功的复合型人才。

本教材的编写正是在上述前提下应运而生。本教材以培养学生商务英语信函写作能力为核心，在内容上将英语语言能力培养和商务知识学习有机地结合起来。在培养学生英语语言能力的同时，注重培养学生的动手能力，使学习者在真实的场景下学习专业语言知识，掌握国际商务英语的交际和实战操作技能。

商务英语函电是一门实践性很强的学科，本书作者长期在企业实践，认识了不同行业的企业职工，收集了大量的邮件。此次编写过程中，作者从四百多个业务文档中精选了近百个邮件，这些邮件涉及鞋类、服装、袋子等商品的交易，所挑选的这些邮件均注重语言点与贸易操作相结合。这些邮件根据国际贸易流程分为建立业务关系、询盘、报盘、还盘、合同、验货、付款方式、审证、包装、装运、保险和索赔十二个环节，每封邮件前有业务背景提示，帮助学员增加对业务的了解。在业务操作中，每笔业务、每封邮件内容都是不同的。传统教材内容如出一辙，教师没有真正的实践经验，语言与内容严重滞后。本教材呈现的邮件原汁原味，每封邮件内容新颖，如买方要求报两种价格、出具出货函、催开信用证等，均为原创，邮件体现了现代电子商务英语的特点。实训环节形式多样化，从开始熟悉产品、填制单据到提出索赔等练习生动有趣，符合国际贸易流程操作规范。

本书由福建商学院吴雯副教授负责全书的策划，并与广州番禺职业技术学院吴含副教授负责全书的统稿，全书十二章。具体分工为：吴雯老师负责第一、二、三、四、五、九、十和十一章的编写，并和福建商学院卢成东老师合编第七章；吴含老师负责第六、八、十二章的编写。本书可供高职高专院校、本科院校设立的二级职业技术学院、继续教育学院和民办高校使用，也可作为从事国际贸易工作的专业人士、公司培训的自学参考书。

　　本书在编写过程中，参考了大量的相关书籍和资料，在此也一并表示感谢。

编者

2023 年 2 月

Contents

Module I Basics for International Business Correspondence

CHAPTER I INTERNATIONAL BUSINESS ENGLISH 2
- I. About the Course ·· 2
- II. Guidelines for Effective Business Correspondence ·············· 2
- III. Layout of Business Emails and Letters ························· 5
- Business Link ·· 12
- Skill Training ·· 12

Module II Establishing Business Relations

CHAPTER II ESTABLISHING BUSINESS RELATIONS 16
- Lesson 1 (A) Self-Introduction ·································· 17
-          (B) Highlighting Advantages ·························· 18
- Lesson 2 (A) A First Inquiry ···································· 22
-          (B) A Reply to the Above ······························ 23
- Lesson 3 Contact Customers after Fair ························· 27
- Business Link ·· 31
- Skill Training ·· 32
- Useful Expressions ·· 34

Module III Business Negotiations

CHAPTER III INQUIRY AND REPLY 37
- Lesson 4 (A) Inquiring for Quantity Discount ·················· 38
-          (B) A Reply to the Above ······························ 39
- Lesson 5 Asking to Quote Two Kinds of Prices ················ 44
- Lesson 6 A Tabulated Order Inquiry ··························· 47
- Skill Training ·· 51

Useful Expressions ·· 53

CHAPTER IV　OFFERS AND COUNTER-OFFERS ·································· 55

　　Lesson 7　A Non-Firm Offer ·· 57
　　Lesson 8　A Counter Offer ·· 61
　　Lesson 9　Offering Substitute Material ·· 65
　　Business Link ·· 68
　　Skill Training ·· 69
　　Useful Expressions ·· 71

CHAPTER V　ORDERS AND CONTRACTS ·· 73

　　Lesson 10　(A) Asking to Send an S/C ·· 74
　　　　　　　(B) A Reply to the Above ··· 75
　　Lesson 11　(A) Asking to Send PO ·· 78
　　　　　　　(B) A Reply to the Above ··· 80
　　Lesson 12　Sending S/C and PI ··· 83
　　Business Link ·· 86
　　Skill Training ·· 88
　　Useful Expressions ·· 98

CHAPTER VI　PRODUCTION & INSPECTION ····································· 100

　　Lesson 13　(A) Inline Inspection Reports ····································· 101
　　　　　　　(B) Advising the Production Schedule ·························· 102
　　Lesson 14　Failed in Inspection ··· 105
　　Lesson 15　Asking to Release the Shipment ·································· 108
　　Business Link ·· 111
　　Skill Training ·· 113
　　Useful Expressions ·· 115

CHAPTER VII　PAYMENT ··· 116

　　Lesson 16　Payment Negotiation ·· 117
　　Lesson 17　(A) Proposing Payment by D/P at Sight ························ 121
　　　　　　　(B) A Reply to the Above ··· 122
　　Lesson 18　Settling Balance Payment ·· 126
　　Skill Training ·· 129

Useful Expressions ··· 132

CHAPTER VIII   ESTABLISHMENT OF L/C AND AMENDMENT TO L/C ········· 133

    Lesson 19   (A) Urging Establishment of L/C (1) ································· 135
                    (B) Urging Establishment of L/C (2) ································· 136
    Lesson 20   Amend the L/C with Correct Amount ······························· 140
    Lesson 21   (A) Amendment to L/C ·· 142
                    (B) Amending L/C to Allow Transshipment ···················· 144
    Business Link ··· 148
    Skill Training ··· 149
    Useful Expressions ·· 155

CHAPTER IX   PACKING & MARKING ··· 156

    Lesson 22   Inner Packing & Labeling ·· 157
    Lesson 23   Outer Packing ·· 162
    Lesson 24   Container Loading ·· 167
    Business Link ··· 170
    Skill Training ··· 172
    Useful Expressions ·· 173

CHAPTER X   SHIPMENT ··· 175

    Lesson 25   (A) Shipping Instructions ··· 176
                    (B) A Reply ·· 177
    Lesson 26   (A) Confirming Delivery Date (1) ··································· 181
                    (B) Confirming Delivery Date (2) ··································· 182
    Lesson 27   Asking for Partial Shipment ·· 184
    Business Link ··· 187
    Skill Training ··· 189
    Useful Expressions ·· 191

CHAPTER XI   INSURANCE ··· 193

    Lesson 28   Insurance Information ··· 194
    Lesson 29   Insurance Clause ·· 198
    Lesson 30   Asking the Seller to Cover Insurance ······························ 201
    Business Link ··· 205

Skill Training ………………………………………………………………… 206
Useful Expressions …………………………………………………………… 208

CHAPTER XII COMPLAINTS, CLAIMS AND SETTLEMENT …………… 210

Lesson 31　Claim on Export Carton ………………………………………… 211
Lesson 32　Settling Complaint ……………………………………………… 215
Lesson 33　Settlement on Inferior Quality ………………………………… 218
Business Link ………………………………………………………………… 221
Skill Training ………………………………………………………………… 222
Useful Expressions …………………………………………………………… 223

APPENDIX ……………………………………………………………………… 225

Module I

Basics for International Business Correspondence

CHAPTER I
INTERNATIONAL BUSINESS ENGLISH

Objectives:
After studying this chapter, hopefully you will have some clear ideas about
1. principles and approaches of writing business letters.
2. the usual structure of business letters and emails.
3. how to edit layouts and arrange the parts of a business letter in good order.
4. some knowledge about products and trade organizations.

I About the Course

国际商务英语函电作为国际商务往来经常使用的联系方式，是开展对外经济贸易业务和有关商务活动的重要工具。正确地掌握外贸英语函电的基本知识，并能熟练地加以运用，是经贸英语专业学生从事外经、外贸行业必须具备的职业技能。通过学习外贸实务中各种英文业务函件、传真以及其他文件的写作格式、术语和各种不同的表达方法，学生能够在提高英语水平的同时，熟练掌握对外贸易业务中的基本技能，提高对外贸易业务工作能力。商务英语函电是一门理论与实践结合紧密的应用性学科。

II Guidelines for Effective Business Correspondence

1. 商务电子邮件的写作方法

外贸业务英语信函往往强调一事一信，以免造成混乱。每个重点成一段是一般的分段原则。一般的信函包括开头句（opening sentence）、正文（purpose message）、结尾句（closing sentence）三个部分。表达不同性质信息的信函，应采取不同的篇章结构。从传达信息内容上可分为两大类：直接式结构（direct approach）与间接式结构（indirect approach）。

1) 直接式结构——用于传递令人满意的或中性信息的信函

从建立业务关系到业务的成交，基本上都是这种模式。但是有的信有四个部分，增加了附加信息（additional information）这一部分，主要是写信者有一些重要的事要提醒对方。

环节	建立业务关系环节	询盘与报盘	业务的成交
开头句	1. 信息来源与目的	1. 提及商品	1. 提及信件
正文	2. 自我介绍或产品介绍	2. 索要与寄送商品目录/样品/目录单等	2. 寄送订单或确认订单
结束语	3. 客气的结束语	3. 良好愿望的表达	3. 良好愿望的表达

2）间接式结构——传递令人失望的消息的商务信函，可尽量减少读者的不悦

传递令人不满意的信息时，为避免过于直率而伤害对方，影响业务往来，一般采用"间接式结构"，即把信函分成五个部分：（1）中立陈述；（2）缘由；（3）拒绝或执行；（4）补救方法；（5）客气的结束语。

环节	还盘	拒绝付款方式	要求修改信用证	申诉和索赔
开头句	1. 提及信件	1. 提及信件	1. 提及信件	1. 提及信件
正文	2. 拒绝执行或接受 3. 说明缘由 4. 提出补救方法	2. 拒绝执行或接受 3. 说明缘由 4. 提出补救方法	2. 找出信用证错误 3. 说明缘由 4. 提出修改	2. 发现问题 3. 说明缘由 4. 提出补救方法
结束语	5. 客气的结束语	5. 客气的结束语	5. 客气的结束语	5. 良好愿望的表达

2. 商务电子邮件的写作原则

写信的原则（Writing Principles）已从原来的 3 个"C"（Conciseness, Clearness, Courtesy）发展到目前的 7 个"C"：

Clarity（清楚），Consideration（体谅），Courtesy（礼貌），Completeness（完整），Conciseness（简明），Concreteness（具体），Correctness（正确）。

1）清楚（Clarity）

清楚是英语应用文最重要的语言特点。商务文书应主题突出，层次分明，可读性强。其内容应明白易懂，无模棱两可、含糊不清、陈词滥调等现象。为了表达的清晰性，有时需要附上范例、说明、图示等。例如：

As to the steamers sailing from Hong Kong to San Francisco, we have bimonthly direct services.（bimonthly 有两个含义：twice a month，or once two months）

Rewriting：

We have two direct sailings every month from Hong Kong to San Francisco.

We have semimonthly direct sailings every month from Hong Kong to San Francisco.

We have a direct sailing from Hong Kong to San Francisco every two months.

2) 体谅（Consideration）

体谅，即多从对方角度（you-attitude）出发，理解并体谅对方的需求、愿望、感情，着重从正面、肯定地谈问题，尽量避免从否定角度谈。下面例句中 b) 句采用了 you-attitude，效果就好得多。

a) We allow 2% discount for cash payment.

b) You may earn 2% discount if you can pay us cash.

3) 礼貌（Courtesy）

写商务文书应本着真诚体贴、有礼有节、不卑不亢的态度。表达方式应委婉、积极，措辞得当。尽快答复对方也是礼貌的表现，体现了对客户的尊重。表示礼貌的句型主要有使用 kindly（pls）的句型、疑问句、条件句与虚拟语气等。kindly 句型代替了原先大量使用的含虚拟语气的复合句，成为目前电子邮件最常用的礼貌句型，体现了现代人简洁、快节奏的特点。例如：

Kindly find attached picture of Slipper 3 colors. Pls quote for same.

If you can supply this article, kindly send me a detailed pricelist. Can you send samples to our CATANIA offices?

4) 完整（Completeness）

在商务英语的使用过程中，我们应力求内容完整。商务英语篇章的完整性特点要求商务英语文书涵盖写信人希望收信人做出积极反应的一切情况及问题，或者回答对方来信提出的全部问题或要求。如在报盘时，需要写清商品名称、价格、交货时间及付款方式等。

5) 简明（Conciseness）

简明指的是尽可能用精辟的文字清楚地表达你需要表达的内容，而又毫不损坏完整、具体和礼貌。各种商务信函应当在涵盖各种必须陈述的信息的基础上做到言简意赅、文字简洁，其语言形式要简单、直接、明了，避免使用笼统的、陈旧的商业术语、怪词、难词和长句，尽量多地使用熟悉的短词和口语体词。完整性和简洁性两个特点相互制约，相辅相成。

如目前电子邮件开头句常为：Thanks for your email. 而传统信函则为：We are in receipt of your letter of Dec. 7.

6) 具体（Concreteness）

商务文书应力求具体、明确、形象、避免含糊、空泛、抽象。在给对方做出明确反应或答复对方的要求或问题的信中，尤其需要做到表述具体化。特别是合同、协议、通知、广告和需要做出具体答复的像报盘、询问交易条款、还盘、理赔等的信函中，需要使用具体的事实和数据。在名词和动词的使用上，多使用意义明确的词。

7) 正确（Correctness）

所谓正确，并非仅指语法、标点和词的拼写这些基本要素。商务文书的内容（如事实、数据等）必须以准确的语言和商务套语加以表达，不得出半分差错，否则会给自己公司带来重大的经济损失。

III Layout of Business Emails and Letters

1. 电子邮件

1) 电子邮件的结构

邮件示例

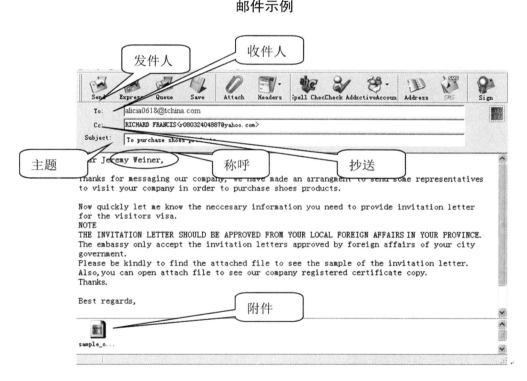

电子邮件主要由信头和邮件正文两部分组成。信头（Letterhead）包括收信人、发信人、主题、日期、抄送对象、附件，邮件正文包括称呼、内容和结尾。

邮件称呼一般为：Dear + 名字，例如：Dear Alicia。尊称用于新客户或者职位级别比较高的老客户；如果双方都是熟悉的客户，交易多年，亦可直呼其名。

邮件主题要有吸引力，力求标新立异，第一时间吸引客户的眼球，例如："The best price list for chainsaw！"

邮件结尾敬辞一般用"Best regards"，"B. rgds"，"Best wishes"。通常在最初阶段的交易中，邮件下方的签名应该完整，包括姓名、职位、公司名称、公司地址、电话传真等。一个标准的邮件签名如下：

Arne Jense

Hong Kong ABC Co., Ltd.

Purchasing manager

Shenzhen Office:

5th Floor, Block C, F 3.8 Building

Tian'an Cyber Park, Futian District

Shenzhen, China

[t] +86-755-87654321

[f] +86-755-87654250

邮箱抄送要注意对方是否还抄送别的人员，如果有，回复时也要回复全部人员。另外，要抄送自己的上司或同事时，要记得在抄送栏里加上他们的邮箱。企业业务一般都有抄送，所以记得要抄送到相关人员。

几乎每封商务电子邮件都会使用附件，因为询盘单、报价单、订单PDF等都是靠attachment发送的，所以在写完邮件后不要忘记插入附件，以免让对方觉得你粗心。附件大小是需要严格控制的，在制作报价单时，插入图片之前可以先用photoshop做好处理，设置图片大小，每张图片都是同样的尺寸，以达到整洁美观的效果。另外附件不要发送太多图片，可把多张图片合成一个PDF文件，这样客户可以一页页浏览，省时方便。如果附件过多，可以根据不同主题分几封邮件发送，这样更加清晰明了。

2) 电子邮件的布局

邮件正文一般不宜太长，以一屏为宜，便于浏览。根据内容不同，长短也不同。最长的可有两屏，最短的只有一行。邮件格式一般有两种：齐头式和缩进式。

(1) 齐头式或平头式（Block Style）

齐头式每行都从左边开始取齐，段落之间一般空一行，签名也放在左下端与每行取齐。目前电子邮件常用齐头式。

Dear Mikhail,

Thank you for your mail.

Our factory is specialized in making outdoor shoes.

There are different 8 outsoles for outdoor product on your sample form. We select some outsoles for your reference. These samples will be sent out March 25 if outsoles be conformed before Jan. 22.

Please see attached and advise.

CHAPTER I INTERNATIONAL BUSINESS ENGLISH

> Thank you.
>
> Best regards,
>
> Celia
>
> (CC: Mr. Benjamin Chan)

(2) 缩进式（Indented Style）

每一段的第一行都从左边空白边缘往右缩进 3—5 个字母的位置，签名放在中间偏右下方。缩进式一般用于平时书信或传真。

> Dear Mikhail,
>
>   Thank you for your mail.
>
>   Our factory is specialized in making outdoor shoes.
>
>   There are 8 different outsoles for outdoor product on your sample form. We select some outsoles for your reference. These samples will be sent out March 25 if outsoles are confirmed before Jan. 22.
>
>   Please see attached and advise.
>
>   Thank you.
>
>   Best regards,
>
>   Celia
>
>   (CC: Mr. Benjamin Chan)

2. 商务信函

1）商务信函的结构

一封商业书信通常由十四个部分构成：七个必要部分（Essential Parts）和七个可选部分（Optional Parts）。必要部分是一封信函必须包括的内容，而可选部分则是在写信时可以根据需要适当增加的内容。各个部分参见下页缩进式信函的标注。

Essential Parts	Optional Parts
The letterhead（信头）（1）	The attention line（交由）（11）
The date（日期）（2）	The subject line（事由）（5）
The inside address（封内地址）（3）	The references（编号）（10）
The salutation（称呼）（4）	The enclosure（附件）（9）
The body of the letter（正文）（6）	The carbon copy notation（抄送）（12）
The complimentary close（结尾敬语）（7）	The postscript（附言）（13）
The signature（签名）（8）	The reference notation（经办人代号）（14）

2) 商务信函的布局

商务信函的格式通常使用缩进式或齐头式。

(1) 缩进式的要领在于信头和事由居中，日期、结尾敬语、签名和寄信人职务都靠右或偏右，而封内地址和称呼则靠左。正文每段开始要缩进若干个英文字母。

上海太平洋贸易有限公司
SHANGHAI PACIFIC TRADING CO., LTD. (1)
Add: 108 LAOSHANG ROAD SHANGHAI, CHINA

==

Tel: 86-21-64875348   Your Ref: JH/nb
Fax: 86-21-64675346   Our Ref: SM/L02-0031   (10)
Email: heilight@public.bct.com

==

                                     Date: September 2, 2022 (2)

To:
S. M. Trading Co., Ltd.
403 Jalan Street, Toronto, Canada   (3)
ATTN: Mr. M. Yasin Marlic   (11)

Dear Sirs,   (4)
                    <u>Re: New Design Brown Bear</u>   (5)
    Thank you for your email expressing your interest in our products.
    We also send a sample under separate cover and we are sure that you will be satisfied with their fine quality.   (6)

                                   Yours faithfully,   (7)
                     SHANGHAI PACIFIC TRADING CO., LTD.
                                      刘世元   (8)
                                   Sales Manager

CC : our branch office   (12)
Encl. Sample   (9)
P.S. The sample will be sent to you on Sep. 10.   (13)
HW/JZ   (14)

(2) 齐头式每行都从左边取齐，段落之间一般空一行，签名也放在左下端与每行取齐。

中 国 包 装 进 出 口 福 建 公 司
CHINA PACKAGING IMPORT & EXPORT FUJIAN COMPANY

ATTN TO: Mr. Hudson　　　　　　　　　Tel: (0755)78560788(EXT)
FAX NO.: 74829402　　　　　　　　　　Fax: 78561115

Date: September 2, 2015
Wongsheng & Co.
Rm 509-511 Tongle Bldg
Shennan Rd, Shenzhen, China
Dear Sirs,

Re: Autumn-2015 Guangzhou Fair

We shall visit your Autumn-2015 Chinese Export Commodities Fair. Kindly let us have the following information:
1. Your Hall Number and Room Number at the fair.
2. Can you furnish us with some sample toys for free distribution?
3. The date on which we will visit your head office in Shanghai.

We await your reply with keen interest.
Yours faithfully,
China Packing Imp./Exp. Fujian Co.

CC J. B. Anderson
EL/JA.

目前信函还会使用，但是主要是在出具受益人证明或质量证明中使用，例如：

受益人证明

DALIAN TAISHAN SUITCASE & BAG CO., LTD.

66 ZHONGSHAN ROAD DALIAN 116001, CHINA
TEL:86-411-84524789

BENEFICIARY'S CERTIFICATE

AUG. 24, 2018 to AUG. 28, 2018

INVOICE NO. TSI0801005

DATE: AUG. 5, 2018

TO WHOM IT MAY CONCERN:

WE HEREBY CERTIFY THAT ONE SET OF COPIES OF SHIPPING DOCUMENTS HAS BEEN SENT TO APPLICANT WITHIN 5 DAYS AFTER SHIPMENT.

DALIAN TAISHAN SUITCASE & BAG CO., LTD.

张平

(3) 信封的写法

写信封的三个重要要求是正确、字迹清楚和美观。信封写法和封内地址写法完全一样，可用缩进式或齐头式。"保密"字样可放在左下端，但通常是放在发信人地址的下端。

SHANGHAI PACIFIC TRADING CO., LTD.
108 LAOSHANG ROAD
SHANGHAI, China

(Stamp)

Mr. M. Yasin Marlic
S. M. Trading Co., Ltd.
403 Jalan Street,
Toronto, Canada

(Registered)

CHAPTER I   INTERNATIONAL BUSINESS ENGLISH

I. Name a company related to each of following products.

1. Shoes & Accessories
2. Home Appliances
3. Rubber & Plastics
4. Gifts & Crafts
5. Machinery
6. Packaging & Printing
7. Minerals & Metallurgy
8. Luggage, Bags & Cases
9. Toys & Hobbies
10. Textiles & Leather Products

II. Arrange the following in proper form as they should be set out in an email.

> Best regards, Dear Tom, The Splenia International Co.（写信人公司）, Mike, tom@hotmail.com, mike@jenny.com

The message:

　　We thank you for your email of March 16 enquiring for the captioned goods.

　　The enclosed booklet contains details of the Table Cloth and will enable you to make a suitable selection.

　　We look forward to receiving your specific enquiry with keen interest.

From:
To:
Subject:

Business Link

China National Agricultural Development Group Co., Ltd. 中国农业发展集团有限公司
China National Chemical Co., Ltd. 中国化工集团有限公司
China MEHECO Corporation 中国医药保健品有限公司
China Metallurgical Group Corporation 中国冶金科工集团有限公司
China Ocean Shipping Agency Co., Ltd. 中国外轮代理有限公司
China COSCO Shipping Co., Ltd. 中国远洋海运集团有限公司
Guangxi Metals & Minerals I/E Group Co., Ltd. 广西五金矿产进出口集团有限公司
Guangdong Textiles Imp. & Exp. Co., Ltd. 广东省纺织品进出口股份有限公司

Skill Training

Exercise I. Getting familiar with the products.
Read this advertisement for trade fairs in Shanghai.

Shanghai International Trade Shows			
Furniture show	March 7-11	Food Show & Beverage	June 11-14
Electronics Spring Show	March 20-24	Packaging Industry Show	June 19-23
Cycle Show	March 29-April 2	Telecommunications Show	September 15-18
Sporting Goods Show	April 13-16	Textile & Apparel Show	September 24-27
Gift & Stationery Show	April 21-24	Toy Show	October 2-5
Automobile/Motorcycle Show Parts & Accessories Show	May 15-18	Electronics Show	October 10-14
Computer Show	June 2-6	Medical Equipment Show	November 18-20
Organizer: Council for the Promotion of International Trade (CCPIT) Jinling Mansions, 28 Jinling Road (West), Shanghai Tel: 86-21-53060228 Fax:86-21-63869915		Venue: Shanghai World Expo Exhibition & Convention http://www.cpitsh.org/cpitsh/ Email: info@cpitsh.org	

CHAPTER I   INTERNATIONAL BUSINESS ENGLISH

Which trade fairs would have products like these? Give names and dates.

1. _____

   _____

2. _____

   _____

3. _____

   _____

4. _____

   _____

Exercise II. Work in small groups. Choose one of the companies and prepare a presentation about the company and its products. Invent any information you wish.

Tianjia Textile Printing & Dyeing Imp. & Exp. Co., Ltd.									
Age Group:	Adults	Product Type:	Blouses & Tops	Gender:	Women
Supply Type:	OEM Service	Material:	Polyester / Cotton	Fabric Type:	Dobby
Sleeve Style:	Short Sleeve	Top Type:	Tank Top	Technics:	Plain Dyed
Feature:	Eco-Friendly	Style:	Casual	Season:	Summer
Place of Origin:	China	Brand Name:	O&E	—	—

Dongguan Arts & Crafts Co., Ltd.
Butterfly Hair Accessory 
Fashion Hair Accessories   1) Material: alloy, crystal   2) Design: according to customers' requirements or samples   3) In a variety of designs and drawings   4) Electroplating: gold, silver, etc.   5) Nickle and lead free

Module II

Establishing Business Relations

CHAPTER II
ESTABLISHING BUSINESS RELATIONS

Objectives:

After learning this chapter, you will

1. be able to get information of foreign firms through different channels.
2. be able to write letters on establishing business relations.
3. be familiar with some business types and trade workers.
4. be familiar with some useful expressions in establishing business relations.

Introduction

　　随着我国加入 WTO，对外贸易不断加强，建立业务关系在对外贸易领域里是一项十分重要的工作。客户广泛，做生意的机会就多。在整个外贸出口的销售过程中，当业务员完成对自身公司和产品的了解、做好定位后，就要有的放矢进行业务开发了。买卖双方相距遥远，我们可以通过以下几个渠道获得信息：

　　1. 广交会及其他国内外展会
　　2. 通过搜索引擎，利用聊天工具、电子邮件等交流方式进行接洽和交往
　　3. 同业商行
　　4. 商务参赞处
　　5. 国内国外商会
　　6. 广告，银行、贸易行名录等

　　老一辈的外贸人员把广交会当作认识客人的最重要的渠道，虽然目前电子商务的崛起使得 B2B 这一渠道逐渐与展会并行，但是广交会或其他国内外展会仍是业务员获得客户的最佳途径之一。在展会上，来自世界各地的商人直接来到你的摊位，跟你交流，询问产品和价格，互相交换名片，顺利的甚至当场成交。展会可根据产品性质分类，比较大的有：美国拉斯维加斯国际服装展览会、美国纽约国际塑料展览会、意大利博洛尼展览会、中国香港国际玩具礼品展、德国慕尼黑国际电子展等。国内目前规模最大、存在时间最长的是广交会，但是义乌小商品市场、厦门每年举办的中国国际投资贸易洽谈会等也颇具影响力，吸引了大批国内外的客人。

CHAPTER II ESTABLISHING BUSINESS RELATIONS

电子商务是国际贸易不可阻挡的趋势，企业既可与著名的电子商务网站（如阿里巴巴、中国制造网、敦煌网等）合作获得客户，亦可通过搜索引擎寻找客户。

Writing Strategy

一、邮件主题

邮件给的主题要有吸引力，力求标新立异，第一时间吸引客户的眼球。

二、开头句

开头句简洁带过证明你是专业而老练的商人，可立即拉近与客户的距离。应避免主动过多地介绍自己。

三、正文

简洁开头后，可立即进入正文。正文亦要简洁，突出自身优势，因为客户最关心的无非是产品规格与价格。所报的价应与现有市场行情相吻合，价太低，客户会认为你不是做该行的，不会理你；价太高会吓跑客户。所以切勿乱报价，而应了解清楚再报价，对于新产品和外贸公司来说这点尤其重要。

四、附件问题

第一次联系客户时，除非客户在询盘中提出，最好不要主动附上图片，或者在附件中带报价单，以免邮件被删除或被拦截。

附件中的内容应给自己的公司做重点介绍，突出产品性能和所拥有的各项认证，巧妙地应用电子版的 CATALOG 和 PRICELIST。

Lesson 1

(A) Self-Introduction

目前各国贸易往来频繁，获得彼此信息的渠道较多，贸易属企业市场行为，因此自我介绍时可淡化信息来源，简单提一句即可直奔主题。第一次主动联系客户时，应向买方介绍公司经营的产品、产品的优势（款式和价格），让客户产生兴趣。

From: Jessy
To: Mike
Subject: promotional and hand bags

Mike,

Thank you for your company information on alibaba.com via private message. Glad to know that you are in the market for promotional and hand bags.

We are a professional manufacturer specializing in producing all kinds of bags with good quality and reasonable price. Materials can be PVC, PU canvas, microfiber, and nylon, with a wide range of colors and styles. Our product line includes cosmetic, school, sports, shoulder, cooler, travel, beach, promotional and hand bags. OEM/ODM is welcome.

Here attached some current hot-selling items with best price for your reference. I will send you factory audit report and 3rd party testing report in other separate emails soon.

Should you have any questions, pls do not hesitate to contact me. Free samples will be sent for your evaluation!

Best regards,
Jessy
Fuzhou Smith Global Bag Co., Ltd.
TEL: 86-591-12345678
FAX: 86-591-12345678
SKYPE: Jessy Liu

(B) Highlighting Advantages

行业内的客户一般会比较关心产品的质量、工厂产品的市场销售情况、质量认证书等重要信息，因此你需要让对方知道你们公司以及产品的优势和特点，例如设备情况、技术力量、行业经验、公司的实力等，以进一步增强客户的信心。

CHAPTER II ESTABLISHING BUSINESS RELATIONS

From: Jessy
To: Mike
Subject: promotional and hand bags

Mike,

How are you? Hope everything is ok with you all along.

We have passed the factory audit from 3rd party. Attached please find the report. We have full confidence in meeting your quality level.

By the way, kindly find our advantages below.
1) Having cooperated with a lot of importers from Europe for more than 10 years.
2) Quick delivery time in 25-30 days (FOB Fuzhou).
3) Own designing team for new products' development.
4) Our monthly capacity: 100,000 PCS.
5) Factory audited by SGS, INTERTEK & WAL-MART.

Any further questions, please do not hesitate to contact us!

Best regards,
Jessy
Fuzhou Smith Global Bag Co., Ltd.
Tel: 86-591-12345678
Fax: 86-591- 12345678
Email: Jessy@hotmail.com
Website: http: //www.Smithbag.com

1. Alibaba.com 阿里巴巴国际站

阿里巴巴国际站是全球专业的国际外贸出口、B2B 跨境贸易平台，为数千万网商提供海量商机信息和便捷安全的在线交易市场，也是商人们以商会友、真实互动的社区平台。商家只需交点费用，即可获得一些买家询盘，反过来亦同。

2. via *prep.* 经由（某地），通过（手段等）

We have sent you via airmail a parcel of the sample cutting. 我们已给你们航邮了一包剪样。

3. be in the market for 想要购买

We are in the market for groundnuts. 我们想要购买花生仁。

in the market 要买或卖

Please advise us when you are in the market. 需要购买请通知我们。

4. manufacturer 生产商

目前根据业务类型（business types），境外客户的分类主要有：中间商（middleman/broker）、批发商（wholesaler）、零售商（retailer）和生产商（manufacturer）。

manufacture *v.* 生产

We manufacture various types of machine tools. 我公司生产各种型号的机床。

5. specialize/expert in 专营

We have been specializing in the export of leather products for many years.
我们已经专营皮革产品出口很多年了。

6. range *n.* 范围，界限；（一）系列，（一）种，（一）类

a wide range of 大量的，广泛的，多种多样的

a full range of samples 一整套样品

My education has given me a wide range of background knowledge in the field of international trade. 学校教育使我获得了广泛的国际贸易知识。

7. line *n.* 行业；货色

We have been for many years in the chemical line. 我们多年从事化工行业。

This is a good line of hardware. 这是上好的金属制品。

business lines 经营范围

8. OEM 原始设备制造商

ODM 原始设计制造商

OBM 原始品牌制造商

OEM（即 ORIGINAL EQUIPMENT MANUFACTURER）意为"原始设备制造商"，即贴牌加工。ODM（即 ORIGINAL DESIGN MANUFACTURER）意为"原始设计制造商"，即设计代工。OBM（即 ORIGINAL BRAND MANUFACTURER）意为"原始品牌制造商"，即代工厂经营自有品牌。

9. attach *v.* 附上

Attached some photos for your review for our hot-selling items.
附上一些图片供您参考，都是我们的热卖产品。

attachment *n.* 附件

CHAPTER II ESTABLISHING BUSINESS RELATIONS

10. hot-selling items 畅销产品

类似的还有：ready seller，quick selling products。

11. for your reference 供你方参考

类似的还有：for your examination/information/consideration/record。

Some samples and pamphlets have been sent under separate cover for your reference.
已另邮一些样品和小册子供你方参考。

A sample is enclosed for your reference. 随函敬附样本供贵公司参考。

12. factory audit 验厂报告

The 3d party factory audit report and testing report will be sent to you soon.
第三方验厂报告和测试报告会尽快发给您。

13. evaluation *n.* 评估，评价

The product needs an expert evaluation. 这种产品需要专家评估。

evaluate *v.* 评估，评价

Would you like to evaluate our samples in advance? 您想先看看我们的样品吗？

It is hard to evaluate the possible results of negotiation in advance.
很难事先评价谈判的结果。

14. kindly *adv.* 商业信函中表示请求的礼貌用词

Kindly send me the price, the models and the pictures of your products if you can.
请把产品的价格、模型及图片寄给我方。

Kindly check and give us final approval ASAP. 请查看并尽快确认最终版。

I. Translate the following expressions into Chinese or vice versa.

1. manufacturer
2. hot-selling items
3. specialize in
4. ODM
5. a wide range of
6. 合理的价格
7. 供你方参考
8. 评估
9. 经营范围
10. 设计团队

II. Fill in the blanks with proper prepositions.

> Dear Judy,
>
> Glad to know your email _____ website.
>
> We supply all kinds of hand tools to global market with good quality and reasonable price, and are very familiar _____ ANSI, BS, DIN, NF & JIS tool standards.
>
> Per my visiting your company web, I found that you have several chain stores _____ Europe, US and Japan. It is our pleasure to find a way to cooperate _____ you.
>
> Here attached some photos _____ our showroom and some current hot-selling items.
>
> Best regards,
> Shirley Cheng

III. Translate the following sentences into English.

1. 我们从中国制造网上获知你方的名称和地址。
2. 我们是一家制造商，专营纺织品进出口业务。
3. 我们有在英国热销的运动鞋款式的图片。
4. 我们的经营范围包括一系列彩色提包。
5. 稳定的交货期是我公司的一项重要优势。
6. 我们已经和世界上一百多个国家的商号合作多年。

Lesson 2

(A) A First Inquiry

一般询盘（general inquiry）是买方想对卖方所提供的产品或商品进行大概了解，会要求卖方寄送目录和价格单等。一般询盘常包括初次询盘（first inquiry），初次询盘是买方第一次写邮件给卖方，因此开头句常有信息来源或者在文中有对自己公司的介绍。

CHAPTER II ESTABLISHING BUSINESS RELATIONS

From: Pagapa
To: who it may concern
Subject: sales inquiry

Dear sir/madam,

How are you?

We got your particulars from the Internet and are glad to contact your company. We are a joinery company based in Lithuania. Our company is looking for suppliers of slippers (beach slippers and etc.).

We want to cooperate with your company. Our company would like to receive your product catalog with photos and prices.

Also, I would like to brief you about our company: RIVONA company has been dealing with foodstuffs import and distribution in Lithuania since 1993. There are three departments: import, wholesale trade and transport dealing with international, local transportation and forwarding agency. The subsidiary owns Supermarkets Chain of 120 supermarkets named NORFA (number 3 in Lithuania, see www.norfa.lt). If you need more information about our company, please contact us.

Thank you and waiting for your reply.

Have a nice day!

Best regards,
Pagapa

(B) A Reply to the Above

工厂（manufacturer）与贸易公司（trading company）还是有区别的，各有优缺点。现在越来越多的国际采购商倾向于向中国制造商采购，以取得价格优势。而贸易公司自己没有工厂，全中国的工厂都可以是贸易公司的工厂。客户需求常常是多样化的，单个工厂往往难以满足客户的需求，贸易公司的优势在于能最大限度地整合工厂的优势，实现客户的需要。

From: Jessy
To: Pagapa
Subject: e-catalog & company profile

Pagapa,

Thank you for your inquiry for our products. Your detailed company and market information impressed us deeply. Hope we can establish long-term business relationship and expand business in the future.

This is Jessy from Fuzhou Smith Garment Co., Ltd. From now on, I will help to follow up your orders. Attached is our e-catalog with photos and prices for your reference!

But frankly speaking, we're a trading company. Our company was established in 2001 and has specialized in this line for more than twelve years. Our products are mainly exported to EU and US, and we are familiar with the quality & testing issue of these markets. Please find our company profile in the attachment.

We are ready to provide more information and samples as requested.

Best regards,
Jessy

1. **inquiry**（英：enquiry）*n.* 询价，询购，询盘
   first inquiry 初次询盘 general inquiry 一般询盘
   make（or: send, give, fax）an enquiry to sb. for sth. 向某人询购某种商品
   They send us an enquiry for our "Cool" Brand Air Conditioner.
   他们来信给我们询购"凉爽"牌空调。
   enquire（或 inquire）*v.* 询购，询问
   We are writing you to inquire the current price of gloves of high quality.
   我们特写信询问有关高质量手套的时价。

CHAPTER II　ESTABLISHING BUSINESS RELATIONS

2. look for/to 寻购……（询盘常用句子）

We look to buy alarm clocks. 我们要购买闹钟。

We are a Mexican company looking for badmintons.

我们是一家墨西哥公司，寻购羽毛球。

3. RIVONA company 立陶宛的一家公司

RIVONA company 是立陶宛第二大零售商，全名是 Norfos Mazmena，控股 RIVONA，在俄罗斯、乌克兰、拉脱维亚、爱沙尼亚都有分店。

4. catalog 是 catalogue（目录）的缩写

Kindly send us your detailed catalog. 请寄给我方详细的目录。

5. distribution *n.* 分布，散布；销售量

They could not agree about the distribution of the profits.

他们无法就利润分配一事达成协议。

distributor *n.* 批发公司，批发商，分发者

The Canadian company yesterday announced a distribution agreement with Digital China, the country's leading IT distributor.

这家加拿大公司昨日宣布，与中国领先的分销商神州数码达成分销协议。

But to sell the wine, you need a good relationship with a distributor/importer.

不过，要想把酒卖出去，你就得跟某个分销商或者进口商建立良好的关系。

6. wholesale *vt.* 批发

　　　　　　adj. 批发的，整批卖的；大规模的

　　　　　　vi. 经营批发业；批发售出

I am in the wholesale trade. 我做批发生意。

Warehouse clubs allow members to buy goods at wholesale prices.

仓储式会员店允许会员以批发价购买商品。

境外贸易商主要有中间商（broker）、批发商（wholesaler）、零售商（retailer）和分销商（distributor）等。

类似的词汇还有：supplier（供货商），dealer（经销商）。

7. forwarding agency 货运代理，简称货代。

8. subsidiary *n.* 子公司；附属者，附属品

The company placed much money in its foreign subsidiary.

那家公司向国外的子公司投下巨额资金。

9. as requested 按照要求

类似的还有：as agreed, as arranged, as contracted。

I. Translate the following expressions into Chinese or vice verse.

1. look for
2. subsidiary
3. expand business
4. OEM
5. foodstuffs

6. 零售商
7. 最新的目录
8. 追踪订单
9. 服装公司
10. 按照要求

II. Choose the best answer.

(　　) 1. We get your name and address _____ alibaba.com.
   A. with   B. via   C. on   D. for

(　　) 2. If you can supply this article, kindly _____ me a detailed pricelist.
   A. sending   B. sent   C. to send   D. send

(　　) 3. We are a Sino-Korean corporation _____ silk clothes.
   A. handling in   B. trading   C. specializing   D. dealing in

(　　) 4. We are looking _____ furniture.
   A. with   B. from   C. up   D. for

(　　) 5. One of our clients _____ Chinese black tea.
   A. in the market for   B. are in the market for
   C. is in the market for   D. be in the market for

(　　) 6. Pls provide me _____ a catalog including all different styles needed for new houses.
   A. to   B. with   C. for   D. on

(　　) 7. We are a company based _____ Germany.
   A. on   B. in   C. from   D. to

(　　) 8. Attached is our e-catalog _____ your reference.
   A. to   B. with   C. for   D. on

III. Translate the following sentences into English.

1. 我是来自广东纺织品进出口公司的销售代表林强。
2. 我们公司成立于 2003 年，拥有员工 300 人。
3. 我们公司有三个部门：研发部、销售部和财务部。

CHAPTER II   ESTABLISHING BUSINESS RELATIONS

4. 我们在寻购 2023 年款的背包。
5. 我们希望能建立长期的业务关系。

Lesson 3

Contact Customers after Fair

I. Contact Customers

参加展会是很多公司选择推广产品的一种很重要的渠道。展会之后，公司会把展会上取得的名片进行分配，各个业务员运用自己的方式去联系客户，业务员必须第一时间跟进客户，简单给客户提供相关信息并根据展会上的笔记，总结并正式向客户报价。

From: Jessy
To: Sebast
Subject: price of WJ01045

Dear Sebast,

How are you!

This is Jessy from Fuzhou Michael Garment Co., Ltd. We have met in the recent ISPO. Do you remember my manager Michael? I am his assistant. He asked me to contact you. Glad to talk with you.

According to the memo, please find the picture of WJ01045 in the attachment.
Price: USD18.0 FOB/PCS Fuzhou. (Lab test fee is not included.)

If you have any questions or any orders needing inquiry, pls don't hesitate to contact us. It's my pleasure to help you.

Best regards,
Jessy
Fuzhou Michael Garment Co., Ltd.
TEL: 86-591-12345678
Fax: 86-591-12345678
Email: Jessy@tchina.com

II. Reply to the Above

From: Sebast
To: Jessy
Subject: reply & Canton Fair
Attachment: winter collection

Dear Jessy,

Thanks for your email!

Yes I remember your manager Michael & also enclosed jacket style.

Of course I'm interested in this & other similar styles, but for winter 2018 we enclosed our collection.

Maybe we can prepare sth. on next spring or winter 2019.

I have following questions from my side:
—Can you send me more pictures with similar styles & approx prices/min MOQ etc?
—Will you exhibit in Canton Fairs?
If yes, we can meet there & talk details–if not we should arrange meeting in your company in Fuzhou in autumn. Then we can agree on winter styles for 2019.

Waiting for your news!

Best regards,
Sebast

1. **ISPO** 此处指的是 ISPO MUNICH，慕尼黑国际体育博览会
   该博览会每年在慕尼黑举行，是目前世界上体育用品及运动时装行业最大的综合博览会，其展品涵盖了体育产业的所有重要类别。慕尼黑地处欧洲中心，ISPO Munich 是西欧及东欧体育用品的贸易中心。
   Canton Fair 广交会
   中国进出口商品交易会开办于 1957 年春季，简称"广交会"，每年春秋两季在

CHAPTER II   ESTABLISHING BUSINESS RELATIONS

广州举办，迄今已有六十余年历史，是中国目前历史最长、层次最高、规模最大、商品种类最全、到会客商最多、成交效果最好的综合性国际贸易盛会。

2. **memo (memorandum)** *n.* 备忘录

在广交会上，业务员把客户资料记在笔记本上，作为备忘录。每个客户的名片钉在备忘录一页上方，下面记录客户咨询的规格、数量和详细要求等，这是参展的基本常识。

Please distribute the memo to all of the employees. 请把这份备忘录发给每个员工。

3. **lab test fee** 产品测试费用（各种产品测试的费用与项目都不同）

Please confirm that the unit price is included 2% lab test fee and Bluetooth license fee. 报价包含2%的产品测试费用与蓝牙许可证费用。

Lab test is needed. Please make sure your production can pass lab test. 产品需要测试。请确保产品可以通过测试。

4. **quote** *v.* 开价；提出（价格）；报价，报……的价

Please quote us the lowest price for Printed Shirting. 请报印花细布的最低价。

The raw coal was quoted at $15 per ton. 原煤报价为每吨15美元。

Please quote us as soon as you receive our inquiry.
请接到我们的询价单后立刻给我们报价。

quotation *n.* 报价

quotation 后可接 for 或 on，若买方提到卖方已对某货作出的报价时，可用 of。

send/give/make/fax/email/sb. a quotation for/on sth. 向某人报某商品的价格

We should be obliged if you would give us a quotation for the supply of 200 Kitchen Cupboards. 如能向我方报200个橱柜的价格，我们将不胜感激。

Your quotation of Sewing Machines is too high to be acceptable.
你方缝纫机的报价太高，我方不能接受。

5. **enclose** 附上

under separate cover 另邮；另函

也可以说 by separate mail，如附在信里则用 enclose（随函）。

enclosure *n.* 附件

6. **collection** *n.* 系列

Full collection will be displayed at the fair. 在会上会展示所有系列产品。

7. **approx prices** 估价，有时用 estimate。

8. **MOQ =minimum order quantity** 即最小订购量（最小订单量）

后面跟具体的数量，一般公司都会规定最小订单量，达到这个量才可以卖。

9. **exhibit** *v.* 参展

exhibitor 参展商，相对应的是采购商：buyer。

I. Translate the following expressions into Chinese or vice versa.

1. lab test fee
2. exhibitor
3. memo
4. collection
5. MOQ
6. 另函
7. 估价
8. 广交会
9. 报价
10. 一般询盘

II. Complete the following sentences in English with the phrases given below.

attached	to be interested in
don't hesitate to contact sb.	to enjoy popularity
kindly note	to welcome one's inquiry

1. _____ （我们欢迎你方4月2日的询盘）and thank you for your interest in our products.
2. One of our customers _____ （对我们的罐头食品感兴趣）.
3. If you have any questions, pls _____ （尽快跟我们联系）.
4. _____ （请注意）that I'm looking for 500 PCS of jeans to Egypt.
5. _____ （随函附上）the photos for our wooden products.
6. Our cases _____ （很畅销）in the US market.

III. Put the following into English.

1. 欢迎到时来参观我们在广州的样品间。
2. 我们的产品出口欧洲、美洲和日本。因质优价低，深受客户喜爱。
3. 我们有经验操作贴牌生产的订单。
4. 请看附件里的报价单。
5. 我们有信心能拿到美国保险商实验室（UL）认证。

CHAPTER II ESTABLISHING BUSINESS RELATIONS

Business Link

the 115th Canton Fair

Exhibition Time and Category

Phase 1 (April 15-19, 2014)

Electronics & Household Electrical Appliances

Lighting Equipment	Vehicles & Spare Parts
Machinery	Hardware & Tools
Building Materials	Chemical Products

Phase 2 (April 23-27, 2014)

| Home Decorations | Gifs |
| Consumer Goods | |

Phase 3 (May 1-5, 2014)

Office Supplies | Food
Cases & Bags, and Recreation Products
Medicines, Medical Devices and Health Products
Textiles & Garments | Shoes

Skill Training

Exercise I. An inquiry exercise

You work for a German company that sells furniture—Kurt Schiller Gmb H, Freidenstrasse 44, Hamburg Germany. You are interested in importing hand-made sofa-beds from the UK. You saw this advertisement in an English newspaper *The Guardian*. Write an inquiry for Mr. Johann Schmidt, the Sales Manager. Ask for catalogs, pricelist. Use the list of functions to help you.

SO FAST ASLEEP ON SOFA-BEDS HAND-MADE IN PINE
TO OUR OWN ORIGINAL DESIGN
For an illustrated catalog of our complete range of hand-made pine furniture, write to:
The New Art Manufacturing Co., Ltd.
96-98 Wood Lane London WSA 3EU

SLEEPS
TWO

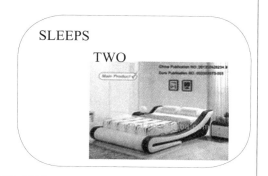

Check list

1) First paragraph: say where you saw the ad;
2) Second paragraph: give information about your company and reason for writing;
3) Third paragraph: request action;
4) Close: ending;
5) Signature: name and position in company.

Exercise II. Fill in the basic information according to the company profile on the next page.

　　公司介绍　　常见于网页上，现在公司简介多数是发布在商务网站上，双方可通过简介互相了解公司的整体情况，或者使用搜索引擎搜索相关信息。公司简介一般

CHAPTER II ESTABLISHING BUSINESS RELATIONS

包括公司概况、公司主要产品、销售业绩及网络、公司发展状况等。公司简介还可以做成 PPT 或 PDF，通过邮件发给对方，这是对外展示自己公司的形象。此外很多客户会主动索取供应商的相关信息，了解公司实力，要求供应商填写供应商表格。表格内容包括公司名称、产品种类、每年销售额、主要市场、是否拥有自己的设计团队和质检人员等，现在请根据如下信息填写供应商表格。

About Us

Established in 2002, Cixi Yongye Furniture Co., Ltd. is located in Cixi city, Ningbo, Zhejiang Province, China with a registered capital of USD350,000. Our company is a professional manufacturer specializing in resin folding chair, plastic folding chair, party chair, event chair and other plastic chairs. With an area of 2,000 square meters and a display room, we now have more than 100 employees and 10 QC inspectors. Our company meets ISO 9001: 2008 certificated by TUV.

With high quality, best service and competitive price, our products are very popular with customers all over the world, especially in the US, Australia, UK, France, Spain, Middle East countries, Africa, etc.

In our factory, there are 10 professional designers. We are good at designing, developing moulds. We accept OEM and ODM orders. We can design and produce moulds according to clients' requirement. We welcome your contact for new product development.

We sincerely welcome clients and friends all over the world to contact us and establish long-term cooperation for a bright future!

Company Profile	Basic Information
Company Name:	
Business Type:	
Product/Service (We Sell):	
Number of Employees:	
Year Established:	

(Continued)

Company Profile	Basic Information
Main Markets:	
Export Percentage:	
Factory Size:	
Operational Address:	
No. of R & D Staff:	
No. of QC Staff:	
Contract Manufacturing:	

Useful Expressions

Opening sentences

1. Having had your name and address from the Commercial Counselor's Office of the Embassy of the People's Republic of China in..., we now avail ourselves of this opportunity to write to you and see if we can establish business relations by a start of some practical transactions.

2. As your name and address were listed in the *International Business Daily,* we are writing in the hope of opening an account with your company.
3. Your name has been recommended to us by the Chinese Consul stationed in your city as large exporters of...goods produced in...
4. We have seen the introduction of your products in the local newspaper.
5. We learn from...that your firm specializes in..., and would like to establish business relationship with you.
6. Through the courtesy of...we have learned that you are one of the representative importers of...
7. Your name and address have been given to us by Messrs. J. Smith & Co., Inc., in New York, who have informed us that your firm has been recommended to us by the Chamber of Commerce in Tokyo, Japan.

CHAPTER II ESTABLISHING BUSINESS RELATIONS

8. We are given to understand that you are potential buyers of Chinese…, which comes within the frame of our business activities.

Self introduction

9. Founded in 1995, ABC Co., Ltd. is a national Hi-tech enterprise in aerosol industry.
10. We are the renowned exporters based in Kerala, India specializing in manufacturing & supplying all kinds of textile floor coverings. Being in this trade for more than 20 years we are proud that we can comfortably meet any customer's demand. We list below the categories we are mainly dealing…
11. Multi-Grace Projects and Services Limited is proudly a Nigerian company registered to carry out business in importation, trading and supplies of consumer home appliances. With active trading in last year, our business has been able to achieve a great feat in the little time of operation.
12. Every year, we develop more than 2500 new designs by professional designers. With novel design, reasonable price, good quality, prompt delivery, all products are exported to America, Australia, Japan, Korea, Southeast Asia, the Middle East and Europe and have enjoyed the great reputation from customers.
13. Located in Longqiao Industrial Zone, Longmen, Anxi, Fujian Province of China, Anxi Lifeng Handicrafts Co., Ltd. Quanzhou is a leading manufacturer specialized in producing small K/D wooden furniture, products, gift items and wooden crafts.
14. With an area of over 200,000 square meters, beautiful environment, standard plants, advanced manufacturing equipment, and a group of senior engineers, Nanxing has established a complete system of scientific research, design, manufacture, sale and service.
15. We are one of the leading importers and wholesalers of various light industrial products in London, having a business background of some 40 years, and are now particularly interested in industrial products of all types.

Module III

Business Negotiations

CHAPTER III
INQUIRY AND REPLY

Objectives:

After learning this chapter, you will

1. be familiar with some useful expressions in making inquiries.
2. be familiar with writing steps in making inquires.
3. be familiar with basic points of inquiries.
4. be able to write business inquiries and status inquiries.

Introduction

在国际贸易中，交易磋商一般始于买卖双方中一方主动向对方发出询盘或发盘。所谓询盘又称询价，是指买方为了洽购某项商品，而向对方提出关于交易条件的询问。询盘内容可以只包括有关货物的价格，也可包括其他一项或几项交易条件。如果买方想对产品或商品进行大概了解，可要求卖方提供商品目录、价格单或样品，这是一般询盘（general inquiry）。如果买方有意购买某种具体产品或商品，在询盘中列明所需货物的品质、规格、数量或交货期，这就是具体询盘（specific inquiry）。具体询盘又包括客户询盘（order inquiry），客户询盘是买方详细地说明订购产品所要求的材料、型号、颜色、尺寸等，要求卖方综合细节进行报价。一般在客户下 Purchase Order 之前，都会有相关的 Order Inquiry 给业务部，做一些细节上的了解。客户询盘是正式开启国际贸易流程的第一环节，收到客户询盘后，卖方应高度重视，做好准确报价回复买方。

询盘时，应注意仔细考虑向哪些国家或地区发出询盘，以及在同一地区要发出几份询盘，也就是与几家供货人联系。在选定了询盘国别或地区后，会选择其中的几家（比如三家）向他们发出询盘，而不是同时向所有供货人发出询盘，因为这样将可能使供货人认为，购货人需要购买的数量很大也很迫切，从而抬高其售价，这对以后的交易会产生不良影响。

询盘一般非常直接，直奔主题，对于询盘应及时答复，有针对性，防止答非所问，以利于交易磋商的进行。

Writing Strategy

1. 询盘信一般开门见山,简明扼要地向卖方了解一般的商品信息。
2. 根据情况说明所要的信息,如索要目录、价格单;希望对方给予一定的优惠条件;或者直截了当说明订购打算,提出所需商品的规格、数量、付款方式、交货时间等,让卖方综合细节进行报价。
3. 期待对方的答复。

Lesson 4

(A) Inquiring for Quantity Discount

买方询问数量折扣也是常见的询盘之一,数量不同则价格不同。大的外贸公司,往往要求报价有一定的格式,就会要求业务员使用固定格式的报价单(quotation sheet)报价。此外买方在订购前往往要求看样。

From: Arne Jense
To: Alicia
Subject: Flip Flops

Dear Alicia,

We are interested to buy Flip Flops. We would much appreciate it if you could email us photo-quotation of the items which we have selected from your booth with all the packing details, individual packing, No. of PCS/CTN, weight/CTN, dely time, competitive price. Pls also email us the individual pictures of those selected items in JPEG file.

Pls quote for qty of 10,000 PCS, 50,000 PCS and 100,000 PCS.
Can we have 2 pairs for testing? If so, we would like to receive two pairs in Size 45 by SF Express on freight prepaid basis.

TRF081174, TRF081175, TRF081150, TRF081142, TRF081180

Will wait your quick reply with all the details and pics.

Regards,
Arne Jense
Hong Kong ABC Co., Ltd.
Purchasing
Shenzhen Office:
5th Floor, Block C, F 3.8 Building Tianjing
Tian'an Cyber Park, Futian District
Shenzhen, China
[t] +86-755-87654321

(B) A Reply to the Above

样品在订单确认的过程中是至关重要的。根据商业惯例，一个订单的落实，一般需要供应商准备至少两次样品，一次是产前样，一次是确认样。这些样品都非常关键，直接影响到订单的进展和将来的合作。所以在准备样品这个环节上，供应商千万不可掉以轻心。

From: Alicia
To: Arne Jense
Subject: Flip Flops

Dear Arne Jense,

Thank you very much for your inquiry to us.

The attached files are the price offering. This price is valid in 30 days subject to the exchange rate or raw material cost or great changes in export tax rebates or other force majeure events.

We usually give a quantity discount of 2% for qty over 200,000 in addition to a 3% trade discount off net list prices. As to terms of payment, we accept TT (30% deposit balance against copy B/L) or L/C at sight.

It is OK to send you a sample for test first. I will check the samples' availability again, as I was told that there were no samples since last week. But we can provide the similar slipper for you, you can evaluate the quality. If you accept, please tell us your Express account and the detailed address so that we can send the samples ASAP.

It will cost USD200 but we will refund the charge if you confirm the order.

We are awaiting your early reply.

Best regards,
Alicia
Fujian Oriental Footwear Import & Export Co., Ltd.

Attachment

Flip Flops Quotation

FUJIAN ORIENTAL FOOTWEAR IMP. AND EXP. CO., LTD.

Add: 9/F MINFA BUILDING NO 88, DONGSHUI ROAD, FUZHOU, CHINA
Tel: 86-591-34567890   Mobile: 86-12345678900
Web: www.orientalfootwear.com   Email: alicia0618@tchina.com

Price Term: FOB FUZHOU   Quotation No: FP12245

Art No.	Unit Price (Quantity 10,000)	Unit Price (Quantity 50,000)	Unit Price (Quantity 100,000)
TRF081174	USD0.88/pair	USD0.76/pair	USD0.68/pair
TRF081150	USD1.80/pair	USD1.60/pair	USD1.53/pair
TRF081180	USD0.90/pair	USD0.88/pair	USD0.86/pair
TRF081175	USD1.30/pair	USD1.10/pair	USD1.08/pair
TRF081142	USD2.60/pair	USD2.45pair	USD2.20/pair

CHAPTER III   INQUIRY AND REPLY

(Continued)

Remarks:
1. MOQ: 7,000 PRS
2. PAYMENT TERMS: 30% deposit, 70% T/T or L/C
3. DELIVERY TIME: after receiving deposit within 30-40 days
4. This price is valid in 30 days, subject to the exchange rate or raw material cost or great changes in export tax rebates or other force majeure events.
5. Packing: 1) inner packing: one pair/box. 2) outer packing: 24 pairs/carton
6. sample fee: USD200; we will refund after you place an order.
TRF081174 TRF081150 TRF081180 TRF081175 TRF081142

1. **qty: quantity** *n.* 数量

   在电子邮件中还流行使用一些由首字母或读音组成的缩略词，如：

   Yr—your   pls—please   ASAP—as soon as possible

   PCS—pieces   CTN—carton   ETD—estimated time of delivery

   PRS—pairs   dely time—delivery time   pics—pictures

   spec—specification

2. **quantity discount** 数量折扣

   trade discount 贸易折扣

3. **appreciate** *v.* 感谢，感激

   We appreciate your kindness. 感谢你方好意。

   We shall appreciate your making us an offer for 800 bicycles.

   如能给我方报 800 辆自行车，我们将不胜感激。

   We shall appreciate it if you will quote us your best price CIF London.

   如果贵方能报给我方 CIF 伦敦最优惠价，我们将不胜感激。

It would be appreciated if you could send us your catalogue and pricelist.

如能给我方寄目录和价目单，我们将不胜感激。

4. **sample** *n.* 样品

通常需要技术部确认的样品有：初样（头样）（initial sample，proto sample）、尺寸样（measurement sample/size sample）、确认样（confirmation sample）、产前样（pre-production sample）、大货船样（production sample）。

此外还有试穿样（testing sample, fit trial sample）、回样（counter sample）等。

5. **SF Express** 顺丰速运公司：民营快递企业，主要经营国际、国内快递及报关、报检等业务。

6. **freight prepaid** 运费预付，由寄件人缴付所需邮寄费用

on collect basis 运费到付，由收件人交付所需邮寄费用

on a basis of 以……为基础

on a barter basis 以易货方式

7. **valid** *adj.* 有效的，确定的

类似的有：good, open。

This offer remains valid/firm until the end of this month. 该报盘保留至月底有效。

We are prepared to keep our offer open until the end of this month.

我们准备保留报盘到月底有效。

8. **exchange rate** 兑换率，汇率

9. **material cost** 材料费，原料费

10. **force majeure** 不可抗力

11. **export tax rebates** 出口退税，export rebates 出口退（减）税

rebate *n./v.* 折扣，回扣，打折扣

price rebate 价格折扣

insurance rebate 保险回扣

12. **T/T** 汇付的一种，业务中常用的付款方式之一，分前 T/T 与后 T/T。

电汇是汇出行应汇款人的申请，采用电讯手段给另一个国家的分行或代理行解付一定金额给收款人的一种汇款方式。优点在于收款人可迅速收到货款。

13. **deposit** *n.* 押金，保证金，存款

　　　　 v. 存放

We hope that your company confirms the deposit soon.

我方希望贵公司尽快确认押金。

14. **balance** *n.* 收支差额，结余，余额，天平，平衡

　　　　 v. 结算，平衡，称，权衡

balance sheet 资产负债表

CHAPTER III   INQUIRY AND REPLY

balance of trade 国际贸易差额

favorable/unfavorable trade balance 顺差 / 逆差

15. copy B/L 提单副本

original B/L 正本提单

16. refund *v.* 退还，归还；偿还

　　　　 n. 退款；偿还金额

If the shoes do not wear well the shop will refund the money.

如果鞋不经穿，商店将退还你钱。

She took the faulty radio back to the shop and demanded a refund.

她将有毛病的收音机拿回商店去要求退款。

I. Translate the following expressions into Chinese or vice versa.

1. proto sample　　　　　　6. 运费预付
2. measurement sample　　　7. 复制样品
3. exchange rate　　　　　　8. 提单副本
4. confirmation sample　　　9. 供我方参考
5. material cost　　　　　　10. 押金

II. Fill in the blanks with appropriate propositions.

1. Our quotation _____ 30 tons of Shandong groundnuts is valid _____ 10 days.
2. You can rest assured that the sample will prove _____ your entire satisfaction.
3. We would like to receive two pairs _____ Size 45 by SF Express _____ collect basis.
4. I am completely satisfied _____ your sample.
5. Kindly send us samples _____ airmail.
6. We'd like to place a trial order _____ you _____ 2,000 PCS cotton pillow cases.
7. Our clients are interested _____ your sample.
8. Most products at the fair are _____ no interest _____ us.

III. Translate the following sentences into English.

1. 确认样有效期为 2 年。
2. 我公司有意从贵公司进口银制品，请寄样品和价格单。
3. 如果数量可以达到一个 40 尺高柜，我们可以给您 10% 的折扣。
4. 一旦收到你们的订单，我们会把费用退还给你们。
5. 随函附寄我们的样本书，请确认。
6. 如果贵方能报女士皮包 CIF 伦敦最优惠价，我们将不胜感激。

Lesson 5

Asking to Quote Two Kinds of Prices

本邮件的交易商品是袋子，国外客户在中国设有办事处，一般客人会要求报两种价格：1) 人民币含税价，2) 美元价。即先国内采购人民币价，赚退税；再自己出口美金价。当然报美元价还可以了解国际市场行情，美元是世界通用的一种货币，外贸通常使用通用的货币报价，以了解该产品的国际市场价格行情。

From: David
To: Jason
Subject: bags

Dear Jason,

I am forwarding you our new amended Lutik logo in the attachment. Our boss has finally confirmed it. As we are going to order bags with this logo, may we ask you to refresh quotation for us?

Please send me your quotation according to our new Lutik logo file for T-shirt bags.

I also ask you to quote us 2 kind of prices : 1) if you will export goods for us, 2) If we will export goods by ourselves, please give us FOB prices for export. We will export all the goods by few consignments. Our total bags quantity will be 650,000 PCS.

Big part of that quantity we will ship to our Moscow office. (1 consignment)

As you said, it will not be possible to send it by usual post because they will not make declaration. Or I did not understand you right? Maybe it is possible also.

CHAPTER III   INQUIRY AND REPLY

The other way, is to send it with others goods in mixed containers which are going to be shipped to those countries, or by express courier service.

Please confirm such a possibility.

If there are any questions, you can contact Mr. Liu for discussion.

Waiting for your refreshed offer.

Best regards,
David

1. **forward** *vt.* 促进，助长；转寄；发送

    We are forwarding you two copies of samples. 我们将给你们寄去两个样品。

    We will forward your letters to him. 我们会把您的信转交给他。

2. **amend** *vt. & vi.* 改良，修改；修订

    Carton size is critical & cannot be amended. 箱子尺寸很关键，不能改变。

    Please amend the L/C and send back to us. 请修改信用证并寄还我们。

    amendment *n.* 修正案；修改，修订

    amendment to the L/C 信用证修改书

3. **logo** *n.* 标示，徽标

4. **order** *n.* 订单，订购；所订货物（后面一般接介词 for，间或接 of）

    We expect you to ship our order No. 25 before the end of this month.
    我们希望你方在本月底之前装运我方第 25 号订单的货物。

    to place an order with sb. for sth. 向某人订购某物

    Should the sample proves satisfactory, we will place a trial order with you for 5,000 dozen. 如果样品令人满意，我们将试订五千打。

    order *vt.* 订购

    order sth. from sb. 向某人订购某物

    We intend to order large quantities of the type form you at the price quoted in your letter of yesterday. 我们准备按你方昨日信中所报价格大量订购这种型号的商品。

5. **consignment** *n.* 寄售，装运的货物，托运的货物

We must ask you to dispatch the consignment immediately.
我们要求你方立即发送该批货物。

Books sold on consignment basis. 图书寄售

They forwarded the goods on consignment. 他们已将该货物托运。

6. **make declaration** 申报

   A declarer can make declaration by itself or authorize any other party to do so under the relevant provisions.

   第三条申报人可以自行申报，也可以依照有关规定委托他人代理申报。

   make tax declaration 申报纳税

   make customs declaration 报关

   make international outbound declaration 国际件出口报关

   make a written declaration 具结

   make documents for customs declaration 做报关文件

7. **mixed containers** 混合集装箱

8. **express courier service** 快递服务

Exercises

I. Translate the following expressions into Chinese or vice versa.

1. refresh quotation
2. make declaration
3. mixed container
4. express courier service
5. usual post
6. 寄售
7. 报关
8. 给我们报价
9. 修改标识
10. 发送货物

II. Fill in the blanks with the following words and phrases in their proper forms.

look for   arrange   show   email   approve

Dear Sirs,

Good day!

I am in Ningbo at the moment _____ a good quality retractable in car charger for Europe market. It also needs to be CE _____. I need it for Samsung please.

CHAPTER III　INQUIRY AND REPLY

> Could you _____ me photo, spec, price FOB Ningbo.
>
> If you are near Ningbo, maybe we can _____ a meeting and you can _____ me sample.
>
> Best regards,
>
> ×××
>
> Company Name: Fonezone
>
> Company Address: 38 Whalley Bank, Blackburn, Lancahire, United Kingdom
>
> City/Town: Blackburn
>
> Zip/Postal Code: bb21nu
>
> Phone Number: 44-1254-654321
>
> Fax Number: 44-1254-654321

III. Put the following into English.

1. 请用人民币报1000套床单CIF伦敦最低价。
2. 请根据我们的新要求给我们寄来报价单。
3. 我们在寻购带丝印（silkscreen）标示的13,000支圆珠笔。
4. 请立即发送该批寄售货物。
5. 我们要大量订购这种袋子。

Lesson 6

A Tabulated Order Inquiry

客户询盘是指买方详细地说明订购产品所要求的材料、型号、颜色、尺寸等，要求卖方综合细节进行报价。一般在客户下Purchase Order之前，都会有相关的Order Inquiry给业务部，做一些细节上的了解。客户询盘是正式开启国际贸易流程的第一个环节，收到客户询盘后，卖方要引起高度重视，做好准确报价回复买方。客户询盘一般采用列表式（tabulated），清楚明了。

From: Henry
To: Alicia
Subject: Flip Flop

Dear Alicia,

Pls see the following below and quote us best price.

Item:	Flip Flops—find attached picture for your reference
Size:	mixed size of shoe 40/42 and 43/44
Material:	Sole: EVA 1,5cm—Black or White
	Toes lace: Plastic—Black or White
Imprint:	1C on top of both soles
Packing:	Each pair in polybag
Certificate:	Phathalate free, skin protected
Quantity:	5,000 pairs (mixed sizes)

PLEASE CONFIRM & INFORM ALSO ABOUT THE FOLLOWING DETAILS:

1. CFS-FOB price/From which Port you ship goods ?
Export Cartons, Weight and Performance of Goods will be checked by our Forwarder before shipment.
Container Shipment will be also operated and prepared by OUR Forwarder !!!
Goods must be transported by truck or train to the port and container get ready for shipment by our Forwarder.
2. Delivery time: 1) Sample lead time ?
　　　　　　　　2) Mass production ?
3. Please tell me packing details: 1) How many pieces are packed in one carton?
　　　　　　　　　　　　　　　　2) Size of carton in CM ?
　　　　　　　　　　　　　　　　3) Weight in KG?

Best regards,
Henry

CHAPTER III INQUIRY AND REPLY

1. **polybag** 塑料袋
2. **certificate** 证书
   Certificate of Origin 原产地证书
   Certificate of Quality 质量证书
3. **EVA** 乙烯—醋酸乙烯共聚物（ethylene-vinyl acetate copolymer）
   由于 EVA 制品具有柔软、弹性好、耐化学腐蚀等性能，因此被广泛应用于中高档旅游鞋、登山鞋、拖鞋、凉鞋的鞋底和内饰材料中。另外，这种材料还用于隔音板、体操垫和密封材料领域。
4. **phathalate free** 不含邻苯二甲酸盐
   azo free 不含偶氮化合物
   nickel free 不含镍
5. **skin protected** 不伤皮肤
6. **CFS** 集装箱货运站（container freight station）。CFS-FOB price 就是 FOB 价中包含集装箱货运站的费用。
7. **performance of goods** 产品性能
8. **forwarder** 货运公司，简称货代，指在流通领域专门为货物运输需求和运力供给者提供各种运输服务业务的总称。它们是货主和运力供给者之间的桥梁和纽带。
   Forwarder cargo receipt showing seller and buyer instead of shipper and consignee is acceptable.
   货代货物收讫收据不显示托运人和收货人而显示卖方和买方，是可以接受的。
9. **container shipment** 集装箱装运
10. **sample lead time**（样品）打样周期
    lead time（前置时间）一般指交货周期，是指从合同签订到出货需要的时间，或是指从订购到供应商交货所需要的时间，通常以天数或小时计算。
    lead time for capacity expansion 扩大生产能力所需的时间
11. **mass production** 大批量生产
    Production processes may be divided into unit production, with small quantities being made, and mass production, with large numbers of the same kind of parts being produced.
    生产过程可分为小批生产（即少量生产）和大批生产（即大量生产同类产品）。

Business English Correspondence (2nd Edition)
商务英语函电（第二版）

I. Translate the following expressions into Chinese or vice versa.

1. order inquiry
2. container shipment
3. for your reference
4. skin protected
5. mass production
6. 打样周期
7. 货运公司
8. 尺寸表
9. 产品性能
10. 集装箱货运站

II. Choose the best answer.

(   ) 1. We are looking forward to _____ your reply.
      A. receiving   B. receive   C. giving   D. give

(   ) 2. We decided to place an _____ with you for pieces of bicycles.
      A. inquiry   B. item   C. order   D. quotation

(   ) 3. We will send the goods _____ mixed containers or _____ express courier service.
      A. on, in   B. in, from   C. in, by   D. on, to

(   ) 4. We are interested _____ kitchen electrical appliances with price range _____ US$3.00 to US$8.00 per PC. Please make your best offer with picture & details.
      A. on, in   B. in, from   C. in, by   D. on to

(   ) 5. If your price is reasonable, we shall _____ an order _____ you.
      A. place, with   B. make, from   C. have, with   D. take, for

(   ) 6. Please quote us your lowest price C.I.F. Lagos, _____ the earliest date of shipment.
      A. stating   B. stated   C. state   D. to state

(   ) 7. If your prices are found _____, we intend to purchase this article from you.
      A. accept   B. accepted   C. accepting   D. acceptable

(   ) 8. Should any of the items _____ of interest to you, please let us know.
      A. is   B. are   C. were   D. be

CHAPTER III INQUIRY AND REPLY

III. Put the following into English.

1. 请查阅随附照片供你方参考。
2. 请告知每个纸箱里装几件。
3. 我们的货代将检查产品数量及性能。
4. 请查阅以下内容并给我们报最优价格。
5. 请确认并告知我方以下具体信息。

Skill Training

Exercise I. Fill in the following forms.

1. There are two forms in making an inquiry. One is letter form, in which the inquiry is made in Lesson 4 and Lesson 5. The other is tabulated form, in which the terms and conditions are made one by one as listed. Now look at the following examples and fill in appropriate prepositions.

Dear Mr. Christina Chen,

Thank you for your company information on alibaba.com via private message. We are a Germany (Berlin) based company looking for a long term partner _____ 20,000 pairs of fashion slipper _____ different colors sizing 38-44 (only rubber or TPU and at least each size one sample 0.12min.) _____ shipment during Aug./Sep.

Your offer should mention usual terms of price, payment, validity, terms of payment, and so on.

Thank you in advance for your corporation and we look forward to your favorable reply at your earliest.

Kind regards,
Mathias Eylers

---

2. Practice: Fill in the blanks according to the above information.

Dear Mr. Christina Chen,

Thank you for your company information on alibaba.com via private message. We are a Germany (Berlin) based company looking for the following products.

Product requirements:
1. Item: _____
2. Size: _____
3. Color: _____
4. Material: _____
5. Quantity: _____
6. Shipment: _____

Your offer should mention usual terms of price, validity, terms of payment, and so on.

Thank you in advance for your cooperation and we look forward to your favorable reply at your earliest.

Kind regards,
Mathias Eylers

Exercise II. You got product details and company profile via alibaba.com. You are interested in TV stand ACT036. Send your message to this supplier. Your message must be between 50-120 characters.

CHAPTER III　INQUIRY AND REPLY

View Product Details: Acrylic TV stand

FOB Price:	get latest price
Port:	Shenzhen port
Minimum Order Quantity:	50 pieces
Supply Ability:	10,000 pieces per month
Payment Terms:	T/T

Specifications

Item No.	ACT036
Color	clear
Material	clear high-quality acrylic
Size	customized
Appearance	fashionable, elegant, exquisite, faddish
Characteristics	durable, easy to clean & maintain, eco-friendly
Package	seaworthy packing
MOQ	50 PCS or can be discussed
Payment Terns	30% deposit and the balance 70% before shipment
Logo	customer's logo is welcome
OEM & ODM	welcome
Port	Shenzhen port
Delivery Time	3-5 days for samples and 15-20 days for lead time, or according to your order

Useful Expressions

1. Thank you for your email of Mar. 15.
2. I wish to extend my appreciation for your kind offer.

3. If your prices come up to our expectations, we would expect to place regular orders.
4. We have seen your cotton garments displayed at Shanghai Trade Fair and have pleasure to ask you to send us details of goods with lowest CIF Vancouver price.
5. Please send us your brochure and wholesale pricelist with terms of payment.
6. Please quote us your best price FOB Tianjin for 1,000m/t Portland cement for shipment in June, 2022.
7. We shall appreciate your lowest quotation CIF New York for 2,500 dz. bed-sheets of the following specifications, inclusive of our 5% commission.
8. We are looking at ordering initially a mix of the above to fill a 40-footer container. Please send us your quote, other specification, pictures and warranty with you company profile and contact details. It would also be helpful for you to provide us info on the present distribution of said tires specifically in North America.
9. Please send us some of your samples to acquaint us with the quality and workmanship of your supplies.
10. Should your price and delivery date be found acceptable, we will place a large order with you.
11. Full particulars as to prices, quality, quantity available and other relative information would be appreciated.
12. We shall be pleased to receive your order, which have our prompt and careful attention.
13. We are quite interested in your products. Please let us know what quantities you are able to deliver at regular intervals. And please quote your best terms of CIF Guangzhou.
14. We are happy to introduce our new branch office to you in the United Kingdom. We are opening a new big fashion shop and interested in the following products of yours, kindly let us have the sample collection, delivery time and total cost for small and large quantity.
15. We are interested to buy in bulk qty Plastic Magic Cube (5.5cm size) customised with our logo printing, pls send photo-quotation with all the packing details, individual packing OPP/box packing, No. of PCS/CTN, weight/CTN, cbm/CTN, dely time, competitive price, pls quote for qty of 5,000 PCS, 10,000 PCS, 25,000 PCS and 50,000 PCS.

CHAPTER IV
OFFERS AND COUNTER-OFFERS

Objectives:

After learning this chapter, you will

1. understand the difference between firm offer and non-firm offer and grasp their relative expressions.
2. be familiar with the terms & conditions involved in an offer and be able to write them independently.
3. be able to make an offer in the form of quotation.
4. be able to make concessions and attacks politely and reasonably when writing counter-offers.

Introduction

卖方为了销售某种商品,一般要按照询盘的要求向对方提供该项商品的信息或者愿意达成交易的有关条件,例如货物品名、规格、价格、数量、包装、装运期、支付条件以及保险等,这个环节称为报盘,又称发盘。报盘有两种,一种是实盘(firm offer),另一种是虚盘(non-firm offer)。

明确、完整、无保留的报盘为实盘。实盘一旦发出,不得随意撤回。实盘往往规定有效期,在有效期内被全盘接受,即达成交易。但有效期一过,该报盘失效,发盘人不再承担报盘中规定的义务。就算受盘人表示接受,发盘人也有权拒绝成交。因此,发盘时,一要明确报盘是实盘还是虚盘;二是明确实盘的有效期,以报盘人收到受盘人答复的时间为准,而不是受盘人发出答复的时间,并须表明以发盘人所在地的标准时间为准。

虚盘是发盘人做出的非承诺性表示。发盘人不受虚盘中所列条件的约束,内容也不及实盘那样完整,无有效期限,但常常注明经发盘人最后确认后方可生效。因此,虚盘实际上和不列明有效期限的报价相同。

商品交易前,买卖双方要对一些交易条件进行讨价还价,实际操作中,有时要反复多次地商谈某个交易条件。这个环节中任何一方做出的答复都称为还盘。

在实际业务中，出口人常用寄送报价单的形式兜售商品邀请对方发盘。报价单可采用印就的格式也可用表列示，后者特别适用于商品繁多的情况。在寄送报价单时，我们应写一封专函，告知对方信内附寄送、报价单，并对询盘表示感谢，或介绍所报的商品，或希望获得对方的订单。

Writing Strategy

一、报盘的写作策略

1. 首先是及时，买家希望尽可能早地得到反馈，这样就要求供应商每天多次上网查询 email，保证第一时间给买家一个答复。

2. 其次是报价的专业性。买家希望和精通产品的人联系，因此卖家在回复查询或报价时，一定要注明产品的规格（specification）。如果你给的答复中对这方面只字不提，或是错误百出，一看就是外行，买家会认为你不是真正的生产厂家，或者对产品并不熟悉，买家的兴趣会大减。

3. 使用电子邮件报价时，不少出口商都会提前进行准备，将各产品的名称、性能、规格和报价做成一张标准的表格。该表格经过技术部门和出口部门的确认，当有买家查询时，可立即将表格作为电子邮件的附件发送，保证了及时和专业的特点，这是一个很好的习惯。使用电子邮件报价时，还要注意根据客户情况定制报价。

4. 分区间和梯度报价。报价内容应尽可能详尽，例如先报 MOQ 的价格，再报 20 英尺柜量的价格或 40 英尺柜量的价格，数量或质量不同则价格不同。

5. 表达对及早收到订单的希望。

二、还盘的写作策略

买方与卖方均可还盘。买方希望价位低，会根据市场定位还价，说该商品的市场疲软；有时则是根据产品和数量要求降价，提出降价的幅度。供应商知道客户想把价格压低，但为了尽快拿下订单，供应商可以要求客人提高数量或者采用类似的材料替代产品，以节约成本。卖方有时由于美金汇率下跌、原材料价格上涨等原因提高价格，要诚恳地向对方说明升价的实际原因，需要征得对方的谅解并得到支持。

CHAPTER IV　OFFERS AND COUNTER-OFFERS

Lesson 7

A Non-Firm Offer

本课邮件回复的是第六课的邮件。邮件回复的特点，有时是新写一个文本，有时是直接在客户的问题后面直接回答，清楚明了，也节省时间。直接在客户的问题后面回复的字体颜色一般是蓝色。下面邮件中用黑体代表蓝色字体。

From: Alicia
To: Henry
Subject: Flip Flop
Attachment: PI

Dear Henry,

I would like to reply to you as per following details. Pls find my reply in blue. This offer is subject to our final confirmation.

...

1. CFS-FOB PRICE: **USD0.50/PR FOB FUZHOU**
   EXPORT CARTON SIZE: 45CM×33CM×56CM, 36 PRS PER CARTON
   NET WEIGHT: 6.00KGS, GROSS WEIGHT: 7.00KGS

2. Delivery time:
1) Samples will be finished 10 days at least.
2) Mass production: **20-25 days after receiving the L/C.**

3. Please tell me packing details:
1) How many pieces are packed in one carton?
   We can make 24 PRS or 36 PRS or 48 PRS per carton. Which way? It's up to you.
2) Size of carton in CM ?

The above carton size: **45CM×33CM×56CM 36 PRS per carton for your reference.**

As there has been a large demand for the items, such a growing demand can result in an increase in price. We advise you to place an order ASAP.

Best regards,
Alicia

1. **non-firm offer/offer without engagement** 虚盘

   虚盘是发盘人有保留地表示愿意按一定条件达成交易,不受发盘内容的约束,也不做任何承诺,任何时候都可以改变、修改甚至取消。因此,虚盘是不受约束的、试探性的报价,其目的在于了解顾客、了解市场。虚盘表示方法如下:

   subject to change without notice 如有变更,不做预先通知

   subject to our final confirmation 以我方最后确认为条件

   subject to goods being unsold 以货物未售出为条件

   subject to prior sale 以先售为条件

   without engagement 无约束力

2. **firm offer** 实盘(或确盘)

   实盘的主要特点是:对发盘人具有约束力,在实盘规定的有效期内,发盘人不得随意撤回或修改实盘的内容。实盘一经受盘人在有效期内无条件地接受,即无须再经过发盘人的确认,就可以达成交易,构成对双方都有约束力的合同。实盘的表示方法如下:

   subject to your reply reaching here before October 2 以你方 10 月 2 日前回复为有效

   offer firm the following on the same terms and conditions 按照同样的条件报盘如下

   offer valid until Thursday our time 发盘至我方当地时间星期四有效

   offer open three days 发盘 3 天有效

   offer reply in ten days 发盘 10 天内答复

3. **offer** n./v. 报盘

   offer 作为名词与动词 make,send,give,cable 等连用,后接介词 for,on 或 of,接 for 最普遍,接 on 较少见。买方提及卖方的报盘时,接 of 为好。例如:

   We are working on your offer of 2000 kilos Black Tea.

   我们正在研究你方 2000 公斤红茶的报盘。

   动词 offer 可以作及物动词,也可以作不及物动词,作及物动词时宾语可以是人,也可以是物,还可以是双宾语。

   We offer firm the following on the same terms and conditions.

   我们按同样的条件报盘如下。

   We will offer as soon as possible. 我们会尽快报盘。

   与报盘相关的表达如下:

   offer sb. sth. at a price 以……价格向某人报盘

CHAPTER IV   OFFERS AND COUNTER-OFFERS

offer sb. firm 给某人报实盘

make sb. a firm offer for sth. at a price 向……报实盘

to accept an offer 接受报盘   to confirm an offer 确认报盘

to decline an offer 拒绝报盘   to entertain an offer 考虑接受报盘

to extend an offer 延长报盘   to withdraw an offer 撤销报盘

to cancel an offer 取消报盘   to renew an offer 恢复报盘

4. **as per** 根据，按照，依照

Quality as per buyer's sample 凭买方样品质量交货

Quality as per seller's sample 凭卖方样品质量交货

As per PP sample 同产前样

details as per attached list 详见附表

Pls quote us as per the attached enquiry sheet. 请根据所附询价单给我们报价。

Please make shipping arrangements as per our order sheet.

请按照我方订单来安排装运事宜。

Please mark the cases (boxes, bags, casks, etc.) as per the drawing given.

请按所给的图样在（盒、袋、桶等）上刷唛头。

per *prep*. 由；（表示根据）依照；（表示比率）每

USD0.50/PR FOB FUZHOU= USD0.50 PER PR FOB FUZHOU

每双 0.5 美元，福州港船上交货。

一些国家货币的表示方式：

欧元：EUR   美元：USD   加拿大元：CAD   人民币：CNY

港元：HKD   日元：JPY   英镑：GBP   澳大利亚元：AUD

5. **subject to** 以……为准，以……为条件

Each list is flexible and subject to review at the end of the day.

每张单子都要灵活掌握，每天下班前要重新检查一下。

All prices are subject to 15% service charge. 以上价格需加收 15% 的服务费。

6. **net weight** 净重

The brand name and the nice artwork need not be changed, but the net weight must be placed on the lower part of the panel.

品牌名字和美丽的图案不用变，但是净重需要放在整个标签的下方。

gross weight 毛重

We'll pack them 10 dozen to one carton, gross weight around 25kg a carton.

每个纸盒装 10 打，每盒毛重 25 公斤左右。

tare 皮重

net price 净价（不含佣金或折扣），"net" 通常放在价格术语后，例如：$50

FOB Shanghai net。

7. EXPORT CARTON 出口箱

Each pair in a box, then 24 pairs of assorted sizes and colors per strong export carton.

每盒装一双，24 双装一坚固出口纸箱，花色尺码搭配。

PACKING: 20 pieces of boys jackets are packed in one export standard carton, solid color and solid size in the same carton.

包装：20 件夹克装一个出口标准纸箱，同色及同尺码的装在同一个纸箱。

8. result in 导致

We hope that our concession will result in a considerable increase in your orders.

我方希望此次让步将来能获得你方更多的订单。

I. Translate the following expressions into English.

1. "联想"牌电脑
2. 永久牌自行车
3. 每桶净重……美元 CFR Lagos
4. 每打人民币 10 元 CIF 香港
5. 每床 15 英镑伦敦成本保险加运费含 5% 佣金

II. Categorize the following expressions. "F" for firm offer and "N" for non-firm offer.

1. subject to change without notice   (   )
2. offer valid until Thursday our time   (   )
3. subject to our final confirmation   (   )
4. subject to goods being unsold   (   )
5. offer firm the following on the same terms and conditions   (   )
6. subject to prior sale   (   )
7. offer open three days   (   )
8. subject to your reply reaching here before October 2   (   )
9. without engagement   (   )
10. offer reply in ten days   (   )

CHAPTER IV OFFERS AND COUNTER-OFFERS

III. Put the following into English.

1. 根据你方要求，我公司就如下货物向贵方报价，以我方最后确认为准。
2. 我们了解到你方市场对 EVA 行李箱需求强劲，随函附上第 555 号报价单，供你方考虑。
3. 兹报盘，茉莉花茶每公斤价格为 1,125 元人民币，神户（Kobe）CIF 价，下周交货。
4. 感谢贵公司对镀锌铁板（Galvanized Iron Sheet）的询盘，现报价如下，敬请惠顾订货为盼。
5. 此报盘以我方货未售出前，收到你方回函接受为准。

Lesson 8

A Counter Offer

要求降价就是对价格条件的还盘，这样的还盘信要给出适当的理由，选择适当的角度。有时买方会通过货比三家来获得最低价，在中国找到几个供应商，然后把供应商的价格发给你，言下之意是我获得的价格低很多；有时则是根据市场定位还价，说该商品的市场疲软；有时则是根据产品和数量要求降价，提出降价的幅度。

From: Mikhail
To: Celia
Subject: counteroffer

Dear Celia,

Good day!

As you know, we are the biggest company in Russia which has retail chain for sport goods. Also we have strong cooperation with many suppliers in the world and in China (especially).

And I was very surprised when I checked your price.

Kindly note we are going to place the order not less than 5,000 pairs per style, but the price must be like following: Style # 825501 and 825492 (Ladies sandals) USD7.00 FOB Xiamen.

Pls reduce your price to our target price.

Kindly note that your first FOB price nearly the same as normal retail price. And our company can not get the profit from this cooperation. (Also there are several questions for outsole.)

In this case I'm waiting as soon as possible your comments, explanation and suggestions for your first price.

Best regards,
Gromov Mikhail
Product manager of footwear subdivision FOOTWEARMASTER company

1. **retail chain (store)** 零售联营，连锁经营销售
   Taizhou Free Space Costumes Limited is a retail chain and the concession to operate the formal professional costumes for the company.
   台州自由空间服饰有限公司是一家以直营连锁和特许加盟为经营模式的专业服饰公司。
   franchise store 指制造厂商授予联营店者经销权的商店
   retail price 零售价　　wholesale price 批发价
   retailer 零售商（包括百货公司、超级市场、商店、购物中心、会员制营销等）

2. **sandal** *n.* 凉鞋；便鞋
   Constant use had fretted sandal strap to the breaking point.
   由于经常穿，凉鞋鞋带快磨断了。
   outsole *n.* 大底；皮鞋的鞋跟
   If the upper appears pulled or stretched so that the foot is sliding off the midsole, or the grooves on the outsole are worn smooth, it's time for new running shoes.
   如果上面的网布看起来呈拉伸或者撑起来的样子，那就说明脚在中底上打滑了，或者大底的花纹已经磨光了，就该买新跑鞋了。

CHAPTER IV OFFERS AND COUNTER-OFFERS

3. order *n.* 订单，订购；所订货物（后面一般接介词 for, 间或接 of）

to place an order with sb. for sth. 向某人订购某物

We are glad to note from your fax of May 28 that you have decided to place an order with us for 100 sets to test the market.

很高兴从你 5 月 28 日传真中得知你们已决定订购 100 套试试销路。

Should the sample proves satisfactory, we will place a trial order with you for 5,000 dozen. 如果样品令人满意，我们将试订五千打。

4. kindly note that... 请注意，需要注意的是……

Pls note that shipment must be made within 10days. 请注意须在 10 日内完成装运。

Please kindly note that the shipment of the order will be effected within 60 days after receipt of your letter of credit.

请注意这个订单的出货将在收到贵方的信用证之后 60 天之内。

5. reduce *vt.*

reduce a price by... 将价格降低多少

reduce a price to... 将价格降低到多少

To close this deal, we shall further reduce our price by 3%.

为达成交易，我们减价百分之三。

reduction *n.* 减少，降低

make a reduction of ... % in price 把价格降低多少

You are requested to make a reduction of 5% in your price to attract more customers.

为吸引更多的客户，请你们降价百分之五。

target price 目标价位

This is out of our target price. 这超出了我们的目标价。

6. profit *n.* 利润

profit margin 利润率

We would like to point out that the prices we quoted are our lowest level, which makes the profit margin very thin.

我们要指出我们已报了最低价，这使得我们只有微薄利润。

7. in this case 在这样的情况下（或 under the circumstances）

I. Translate the following expressions into Chinese or vice versa.

1. place the order
2. profit margin
3. in this case
4. to extend an offer
5. to entertain an offer
6. 零售联营
7. 批发价
8. 批发商
9. 供货商
10. 经销商

II. Correct mistakes in the following sentences.

1. Business is impossible if you make a reduction of 2% in our quotation.
2. If you can improve your price by 2%, we'll place an order with you.
3. Since our products enjoy high reputation in the world market, it is reasonable that the price quoted by us is higher than others.
4. We would like to point out that the price is our lowest level, that makes the profit margin very small.
5. In compliance to your request, we make offers for our products. Our offer is subject to your reply reaching at us before October 31.
6. We offer you per kg HK$3.00 CFR Hong Kong for canned mushroom.
7. We are not available for export.
8. Our company trades in many countries for porcelain.

III. Translate the following sentences into Chinese.

1. In reply, we regret to inform you that our buyers in Rotterdam find your price is on the high side.
2. Information indicates that some parcels of Indian origin have been sold here at a level about 10% lower than yours.
3. We do not deny that the quality of Chinese slipper is slightly better, but the difference in price should, in no case, be as big as ten percent. To step up the trade, we counter-offer as follows, subject to your reply received by us on or before July 1, 2018.

CHAPTER IV OFFERS AND COUNTER-OFFERS

Lesson 9

Offering Substitute Material

为了满足客人的目标价，一个重要的手段就是修改产品的部件或包装，减少长度、厚度或用类似的材料来替代以节约成本，想办法节省成本，降低价格，以达到客户的期望或目标。本邮件中商品是运动鞋，出口商把连体鞋舌改成常规鞋舌，原来车两次改为车一次，可以节省成本，但从外部看又没有太大差别。

From: Celia
To: Mikhail Gromov
Subject: counter-offer

Dear Mr. Mikhail Gromov,

In view of long term business partnership, Mr. Benjamin Chan is willing to accept your target price on following styles. Pls give big quantity per style, so we can have more bargain power against our material suppliers. Our Finance Dept. already complained that our price was too low. Quotation offer to your company does not have any room for price reduction.

In order to meet your target price, we suggest making the following changes.
1) Style # 825501 and 825492 (Ladies sandals)
   a) We accept USD7.00. FOB Xiamen. Box pack.
   b) Outsole: Phylon/Rubber (as per your request)
   c) Gusset tongue: change to regular tongue as used on ROSS style# B7-Y4012-1, see photo B.

2) Style # 826100 (Men sandals)
   a) We accept USD8.00. FOB Xiamen. Box pack.
   b) Upper: stitched construction (as per your request)
   c) Double stitching: change to single stitching. See photo A.

3) Style # 826040 (Youth sandals) and 826081 (Men sandals)
   We are still searching for outsole. Price will be confirmed later.

If you know any info. on outsole suppliers, we will appreciate your advising us.

Please advise.
Best regards,
Celia
(CC: Mr. Benjamin Chan)

1. **substitute** *n.* 替换产品，代用品

    take/accept A as a substitute for B 以 A 代替 B

    To protect environment, we have already used synthetic materials as a substitute for wood in our production. 为了保护环境，我们早已在生产中用合成材料替代了木材。

    No substitutes should be used without our approval. 未经我方的同意不能用替代品。

    substitute *vt.* 代替，替换

    substitute A for B 或 substitute B by/with A 以 A 替代 B

    If the article needed is out of stock, pls substitute it with a similar one.
    如果所需商品无货，请用近似产品替代。

    We agree to substitute plastics for wood. = We agree to replace wood with/by plastics.
    我们同意以塑料替代木材。

    Plastics will be substituted for wood. = Wood will be replaced with/by plastics.
    塑料将替代木材。

    substitution *n.* 代替

    We enclose an amended contract in substitution for the previous one.
    随函附上一份已修改的合同以替代以前的那份。

2. **Phylon** 塑料粒子加热发泡后灌入模型加压冷却形成的材料

    这是一种重量极轻、质地柔韧、造价稍高的材料，因其会产生细小的皱纹而易于辨认。用 Phylon 塑胶粒子先加热发泡再灌入模型加压冷却，表面较白且有皱纹，减轻质量的同时可以给脚部提供持续的缓震，是 Nike 现在最常用的一种中底材料。

3. **Gusset tongue** 舌翼

CHAPTER IV OFFERS AND COUNTER-OFFERS

4. **stitch** *n.* 针脚，线迹，一针

A hole was torn in your jacket. Let me stitch up the torn jacket for you.

你的上衣撕了个口子，我给你缝缝吧。

double stitch 车双线

I. Translate the following expressions into Chinese or vice versa.

1. business partnership
2. target price
3. price reduction
4. per style
5. bargain power
6. 常规鞋舌
7. 车双线
8. 替代品
9. 撤销报盘
10. 还盘

II. Rewrite the underlined parts in the following sentences.

1. Our first-class textiles are <u>enjoying popularity</u> in the world.
2. If the article needed is out of stock, please <u>substitute it with a similar one</u>.
3. <u>In view of</u> our long and friendly relations, we agree to increase the price to USD118.45/PC FOB Qingdao.
4. This is <u>not in line with</u> our target price.
5. We are a specialized corporation, <u>handling</u> the export of animal by-products.
6. Our Finance Dept. already complained that our price was <u>on the low side</u>.

III. Translate the following offer into Chinese.

Dear Mr. Smith,

Thank you very much for your inquiry of July 9, 2016 and we appreciate your interest in our leather shoes. As requested, we take pleasure in making you a special offer, as follows:

Name of commodity: "Lining" Brand Gym Shoes

Size: 35-44

Color: Black, brown, white

> Price: US$28.00 per pair FOB Fuzhou
> Shipment: 30 days after receipt of L/C
> Terms of payment: By confirmed, irrevocable L/C available by seller's documentary draft at sight to be valid for negotiation in China until 15 days after the date of shipment.
>
> We have to point out that the offer remains good for two weeks due to heavy demands in the high season.
>
> We are confident that you will be satisfied with both good quality of our products and the competitive prices. We trust the above offer will be acceptable to you and await your first order with keen interest.
>
> Yours sincerely,
> ×××

IV. Write a counter-offer or an email in reply to the above offer and your letter should cover the following points.

1. Express thanks to the offer
2. Regret the price is on the high side
3. Have a hard time convincing our clients at your price
4. Impossible to accept the offer
5. Make a counter-offer
6. Suggest the way to come to terms

Business Link

make a firm offer for/on 报实盘
give non-firm offer 报虚盘
counter offer 还盘
without engagement 无约束力
quotation sheet 报价单
unit price 单价
E. & O.E. 有错当查
reasonable price 合理价格

CHAPTER IV OFFERS AND COUNTER-OFFERS

workable price 价格可行
make some allowance 折价
make a discount 打折扣
a base price 底价
a floor price 地板价
rock bottom price 最低价
cut the price to the limit 降到最低价
narrow margin of profit 无利可图
no room for further reduction 无法降价
make a deal/make business/come to terms 成交
conclude the transaction/conclude terms/conclude a deal 达成交易
decrease the price/reduce the price/lower the price/cut the price 减价

Skill Training

Exercise: Read the following information and do exercises according to the requirements.

> **Subject:** quote for a T-shirt order
>
> Dear Sir or Madam,
>
> We are looking for a supplier for the below order.
>
> Style: 100% Cotton, 145 Gram, Basic Round Neck, S/S T-shirt, White Only.
> Size: European Size M/L/XL
> Spec Taken: M   L   XL (All in CMS)
> 1/2 Chest: 56, 59, 62
> Length: 72, 74, 76
> Slv Lgth: 22, 23, 24
> Target Price: Per T-shirt-FOB US$0.90
> Packing: 1 PC in a poly bag and 100 PCS in one export carton.
> Qty: Will Be 10 × 40FT Containers.
>
> Pls quote your best FOB price and C&F Lome-Togo seaport price urgently.
>
> Best regards,
> Pinto

练习1) 根据买家信息填写下面表格。

No.	Main Information in the Inquiry	
1	Product Name	
2	Quantity	
3	Target Price (Per Piece)	
4	Style	
5	Size	
6	Spec Taken: M L XL (All in cms)	
7	Packing	
8	The Buyer's Requirement	

练习2) 根据以上询盘信息写一封答复邮件，同时以你虚拟公司的名义，制作一份报价表，寄给买方。

卖方信息如下：

公司名称：中国纺织品进出口公司福建分公司

公司地址：123 Hubin Road, Fuzhou, China   Web: www.fujiantextile.com

Fax: 86-591-87654321   Email: senda@hotmail.com   Tel: 86-591-87543210

注意：(1) 报价时，需要有两个价格：Best FOB price and C&F Lome-Togo seaport urgently。

(2) 报价时，需要加上你报给买家的 delivery time，而这个 delivery time 的时间与工厂报给你的 delivery time 的时间是不一样的。

CHAPTER IV OFFERS AND COUNTER-OFFERS

FUJIAN TEXTILE IMP. AND EXP. CO., LTD.			
Add: ,			
Tel:		Mobile:	
Web:		Email:	
Quotation Sheet			
Quotation No:		Quotation Date:	
1. Description of Goods	2. Quantity (PCS)	3. Unit Rice (USD)	4. Amount
More Product Information 1. Style: 2. MOQ: 3. Sample Terms: 1) Available Sample: USD1/model; the sample cost will be deducted from the total amount of your future order if you place an order in the near future. 2) Available Size: 4. Quality: 5. Packing: 6. Delivery Time: 7. Payment:			

Useful Expressions

Offer

1. Would you please offer us 1,000 sets of computers CFR Copenhagen.
2. Please quote us your lowest price for 3,000 tons of corns CIF Fukuoka.
3. This offer is firm subject to your immediate reply which should reach us not later than June 6, 2011.
4. As there has been a large demand for our products and the rise of raw material, we hope you take advantage of our special offer as soon as possible.
5. We now offer firm subject to your acceptance received here within 7 days.

Counter offer

1. In reply, we regret to inform you that your price is out of line with the prevailing market here.
2. To have this business concluded, you need to lower your price at least by 6%.
3. If you are willing to reduce the prices you quoted by 10%, there is possibility of concluding a deal.
4. If you reduce your price, say 6%, we might make business.
5. Your price is too high for us to accept. As the market is declining, we hope you will consider our counter-offer and respond to us as soon as possible.

Making a compromise

1. We are prepared to allow you a 5% discount if you can increase the quantity of your order to 80,000 pairs.
2. We should fill the gap by making further concession.
3. For the sake of encouraging future business, we may grant you a special discount of 3%.
4. For a sincere desire to increase trade between us, we are going to cut our price by 4%.
5. May I suggest we go fifty-fifty and close the gap?
6. Shall we meet half way?
7. With an eye to future business, we'll make an exception and allow you a 2% discount.
8. If you increase your quantity to 50,000 dozens, we'll manage to make HKD8.00.
9. The utmost we can do is to reduce the price by 3%.
10. Let's make concessions so business will be closed at this price.

CHAPTER V
ORDERS AND CONTRACTS

Objectives:
After learning this chapter, you will
1. learn how to place and confirm an order.
2. learn the contents of a sales contract or sales confirmation.
3. learn how to fill in a contract in English.
4. understand the obligations of the buyer and the seller.

Introduction

在国际贸易中,交易的一方明示接受另一方的交易条件,交易即达成,然后签订具有合同性质的文件。如果买方发出订购信;寄出订单或者购货确认书,要求卖方按上面所列出的条件供货,并要求卖方签回一份,就是对自己订货和对卖方的确认。订单信通常需要明确以下条件:商品名称、质量要求和规格、订购数量、价格及价格条件、总额等。买方通常强调交货时间或者敦促对方尽快交货,根据需要还可能提出付款方式、供现货等其他条件。

买卖双方成交后,可以用函电确认成交。也可以制定销售合同或者销售确认书、订单、购货确认书,寄给对方会签时附上一封短的成交信,对方收到后回信确认并签回一份合同。确认订货信中,要注意重复对方合同中的主要内容,强调支付货款要求,表达对寄去合同予以会签的愿望等。本章提供了一系列订单、成交的信函做范例学习。

Writing Strategy

订购业务思路如下:
1. 开头句:买方首先感谢卖方报盘,表明愿意订购某商品。
2. 中间部分:提到寄出订单、购货确认书或者购货合同。
3. 结尾句:希望卖方尽快会签、发货等。

确认订货的业务思路如下：

1. 开头句：确认信中首先重复说明收到对方有关合同的编号、成交商品的名称、规格及订购数量等。

2. 中间部分：说明寄出销售合同、形式发票或者销售确认书请对方会签。

3. 结尾句：希望买方再订货并尽快办理货款支付手续等。

Lesson 10

(A) Asking to Send an S/C

本课的案例中交易商品为袋子。在国际贸易中，交易的一方明示接受另一方的交易条件，交易即达成，然后签订具有合同性质的文件。买卖双方都会互相要求寄送购货合同或销售合同，合同意味着交易的成交。由卖方按照双方认可的条款制定的合同称之为销售合同，简化形式为销售确认书 S/C（Sales Confirmation）。

From: David @hotmail.com
To: Jason @tchina.com
Subject: purchase order

Hi Jason,

Regarding the samples, pls send thicker ones only if you already have them in stock, otherwise the quality of those you already sent is good enough. I just wanted to check samples with similar thickness to that I am ordering.

I am OK with the terms, 50% deposit and 50% when the goods reach Italy. Letter of credit is also fine for me, if you prefer. Pls send me a bilingual (Chinese-English) contract so we can make our agreement official.

Production time is a bit tricky, if 20 days is too short, let's try to get the bags done within 30 days.

I will visit your factory when we can start production so I can check the bags when they come out of the machines.

When do you think we can begin?

In the meantime I will provide you with the vector file for the print. Good news for you is that I will place another order for a half container in the next days. Specifications will follow.

Best regards,
David

(B) A Reply to the Above

From: Jason @tchina.com
To: David @hotmail.com
Subject: purchase order

Hi David,

Good day to you.

Regarding the similar samples with D2W logo which were exported to Australia, the thickness of bags is 0.01mm. It is just for your reference.

Similar thickness in stock will be prepared and sent to you today. But there's no printing D2W logo in the bag. Pls note it.

According to usual practice, the terms must be 50% in advance as deposit, 40% before shipment and 10% when the goods reach Italy. Or 50% deposit, and the balance 50% use 100% irrevocable L/C at sight is OK.

Now we have more repeat orders to arrange. We are pretty busy recent month. Pls give me enough time for mass production. Thank you.

We are waiting for your vector file for the print and welcome to visit our factory.

By the way, the bilingual contract will be sent via email. Pls wait patiently.

Hope to get good news from you. Thanks again.

Enjoy the weekend!

Jason

1. **S/C (Sales Confirmation)** 销售确认书
   Sales Contract 销售合同
   相关词组还有：
   bilingual contract 双语合同　　　　installment contract 分期合同
   barter contract 易货合同　　　　　binding contract 有约束力合同
   blank form contract 空白合同　　　cross license contract 互换许可证合同
   formal contract 正式合同　　　　　illegal contract 非法合同
   draft/draw the contract 起草合同　make out the contract 缮制合同
   sign the contract 签订合同　　　　execute/honor/perform the contract 履行合同
   break/breach the contract 违反合同

2. **stock** *n*. 存货（后接介词 in/of，再接商品）
   At present, we have only a limited stock in (of) linen goods.
   目前我们的亚麻货物库存有限。
   There are no stocks available at present. 目前无货可供。
   Our stocks are rapidly running short (low). 我们的存货越来越少。
   We have run out of stock. 我们的存货已售完。
   We can supply this quantity from stock (ex stock). 这个数量我们可供现货。
   If you have Fountain Pens in stock, please send us some samples.
   如果你方有水笔现货，请给我们寄些样品。

3. **regarding** *prep*. 关于，至于
   I had nothing to say regarding this matter. 对于这件事我无话可说。
   The proposal regarding safety in production was called up in the conference this morning. 有关安全生产的提案今天上午已在会上提出讨论。
   类似的还有：in/with regard to, with reference to, as regards, concerning 等。

4. **tricky** *adj*. 狡猾的；（形势、工作等）复杂的；难办的；困难的
   The design is a bit tricky. 设计有点复杂。

5. **vector file** 电子文件

6. **specification** *n*. 规格；规范；[常用复数] 明细单，具体规划（或设计）；说明书；（合同等中的）具体事项
   Have you get a product of this specification? 贵方有这种规格的产品吗？
   He conformed the plans to the new specifications.

CHAPTER V ORDERS AND CONTRACTS

他使各项计划都符合新的规格要求。

Replacement is guaranteed if the products are not up to the standard; we undertake to replace the specifications. 产品不合规格，保证退换。

7. usual practice 惯例

As our usual practice, insurance covers basic risks only, at 110 percent of the invoice value. 按照我们的惯例，只保基本险，按发票金额110%投保。

8. repeat orders（或 re-order）续订订单，俗称翻单或返单。

客人下了一个订单，觉得销路不错，就再下一个与上一单要求差不多的订单。这种形式就是翻单。有的订单因为质量好连续翻单。

repeat order 可简称为 repeat，复数为：repeats，repeat orders，further orders。repeat order 与原订单除装运期不同外，价格与数量甚至详细规格亦未必相同。假定除装运期不同外，其他一些条件都相同，则称为 "duplicate order"。

I. Translate the following expressions into Chinese or vice versa.

1. bilingual contract
2. vector file
3. specifications
4. make out the contract
5. ex stock
6. 不可撤销信用证
7. 翻单
8. 大量生产
9. 惯例
10. 销售合同

II. Fill in the blanks with correct forms of the words given below.

1. satisfy

   1) The quality of your new product _____ us in every respect.
   2) We assure you that the goods will turn out to the _____ of your end-users.
   3) We are not quite _____ with the shipment.
   4) We are confident that this order will be _____ to you.

2. regard

   1) In _____ to S/C No. 1360, please ship the goods without delay.
   2) As _____ the balance, we'll advise you the position in a few days.
   3) We _____ this as a good beginning.

4) We know nothing _____ the market condition there.

3. regret

1) We find _____ that you failed to book the shipping space on S.S. "Asia".

2) We expressed _____ at the delay.

3) We are _____ that we can not supply the entire quantity required.

4) It is _____ that the matter should still be hanging unsettled.

III. Translate the following sentences into English.

1. 我们对这批货很满意，现续订 50,000 件。

2. 如果你方有水笔现货，请给我们寄些样品。

3. 如果没有"蝴蝶"牌现货，请告知其他牌子可供现货的规格。

4. 按照我们的惯例，付款方式是 30% 的订金，70% 保兑的不可撤销的信用证。

5. 随函附寄我方一份双语合同，请查收。

6. 这个时候不需要把我们的图标印到样品上。

Lesson 11

(A) Asking to Send PO

PO（purchase order）即购货合同，是买方寄给卖方的正式合同，意味着正式下单给卖方，卖方得到 PO 后才能安排生产，收到 PO 后卖方还要做 S/C（Sales Confirmation）和 PI（Proforma Invoice）给买方确认，把供货细节再确认一下，以免理解不一致。PI 即形式发票，亦称估价单，可供进口商向贸易或外汇管理当局申请进口许可证或外汇等时用，但双方签署后可当正式合同，另外还可作为报价单使用。

From: Celia
To: Mikhail
Sent: Nov. 22, 2018
Subject: new orders for SS10 (WS002 and WS003)

CHAPTER V   ORDERS AND CONTRACTS

Dear Mikhail,

1) Official Order

Have you finalized your order?

Pls issue official PO to us so that we can send S/C & PI to you.

2) Order Details

Pls kindly advise style, color, size and delivery time for each shipment in detail. So we can make production schedule for Sportmaster.

3) Specification

We would like to know when we can expect to receive specification for WS002 and WS003 order.

4) Deposit

As our agreement, pls submit 20% deposit to our company so we can prepare materials in advance.

Thanks and best regards,
Celia
(CC: Mr. Benjamin Chan)

Attachment:

Re-send our company info. as follows:

The Seller: TAIZIN COMPANY LIMITED

Legal Address: RM. 705, 7th Floor Fortress Tower, 250 King's Road, North Point, Hong Kong

Beneficiary Name: TAIZIN COMPANY LIMITED

Beneficiary: TAIZIN COMPANY LIMITED

Beneficiary Address: RM. 705, 7th Floor Fortress Tower, 250 King's Road, North Point, Hong Kong

Beneficiary Bank A/C No. : 004-2-608331

Bank Name: HSBC, North Point Branch

Bank Address: No. 306-316 King's Road, North Point, Hong Kong

SWIFT Code: HSBC HKHHHKH

(B) A Reply to the Above

确认样品后，通常情况下买方会给供货商下订单。一般在接受生产前，买方先交付一定数额的订金给供货商，具体数量由买卖双方协商。

From: Mikhail
To: Celia
Sent: Nov. 24, 2018
Subject: purchase order

Dear Celia,

We are glad to receive your duplicate samples and feel satisfied with them.

Attached is our SS10 Order. As agreed upon, we will wire 20% of the total value to you as deposit through HSBC, North Point Branch.

Since our end-users are in urgent need of the goods, pls arrange production accordingly.

We hope this transaction will mark a good beginning between us.

Best regards,
Mikhail

1. **PO (purchase order)** *n.* 购货订单
    订购函可以是表格形式，如订单、购货确认书或者购货合同，也可以是商务信函。订购函的内容必须准确、清楚、讲究礼貌，对于重要的交易条款必须做出明确规定。
    其他的表达法还有：
    order for custom-made 定制的订单
    outstanding/pending order 未完成订单
    substantial order 可观的订单

CHAPTER V ORDERS AND CONTRACTS

    fresh order 新订单

    routine orders 日常订货

    following up the order 订货追踪

    confirmation of order 确认订单

    standing order 长期订单

    to execute/fulfill/fill/carry out an order 执行订单

    to decline/turn down/refuse an order 拒接订单

    to close/confirm/take on an order/entertain an order 接受订单

    to cancel/withdraw/revoke an order 取消订单

    to hold up/suspend an order 暂停执行订单

2. **finalize** *v.* 使完成；把……完成，使结束，使完结

    We need to finalize the next product launch. 我们需要最后确定新产品的推出。

    Thus, it is essential that you understand what terms you agreeing to before you finalize a contract. 因此，在敲定合同之前，理解你所签订的条款是至关重要的。

3. **as agreed upon** 按协议

    其他类似的表达有：

    as contracted 按合同规定 as requested 按要求 as referred 按所提及的

4. **production schedule** 生产计划，[经管] 生产进度表，产品明细表

    The delayed order scrambled New Flyer's production schedule for the rest of the year, and led to the layoffs.

    这搁浅的订单使得新飞公司本年度的生产日程受到严重影响，从而导致裁员。

5. **be in urgent/great/need of (be badly in need of)** 急需

    We are in urgent need of raw materials. 我们急需原材料。

6. **without any delay** 迅速

    Please rush documents without any delay. 请速寄交单证。

7. **submit** *vt.* 提交；主张；呈递 *vi.* 提交，服从

    In that case we can submit the entry several days after shipment.

    在这种情况下，可以在装运后的几天内提出申报。

    submit an offer 提交报盘

    submit shipping documents 交单

8. **in advance**

    Berths on steamships can be booked a long while in advance.

    轮船上的床位可以提前多日预订。

    We won't deliver unless you pay us in advance! 除非你们先付款，否则我们不发货！

9. **mark a good beginning** 标志良好的开端

We hope this will mark a good beginning of our long, friendly and mutually beneficially business relations. 我们希望这标志着我们双方长久、友好、互利的良好关系的开端。

10. transaction *n.* 交易

   conclude transaction 达成交易

   类似的还有：put the deal through，finalize the business, come to terms。

Exercises

I. Translate the following expressions into Chinese or vice versa.

1. Proforma Invoice
2. official PO
3. as agreed
4. in advance
5. end-users
6. 按合同规定
7. 重复订单
8. 急需
9. 达成交易
10. 生产计划

II. Read the following sentences and fill in the missing prepositions.

1. We are well experienced _____ this line and can place orders with you _____ large quantities if your prices are attractive enough.
2. We confirm the sale _____ you of 100 tons groundnuts resulting _____ letters exchanged.
3. We hope we could come _____ business _____ you.
4. We look forward _____ hearing _____ you again the possibilities of your further orders.
5. We regret that we have to cancel our order because of the inferior quality _____ your products.
6. You can be assured that the goods will turn out _____ your entire satisfaction.
7. Please refer _____ the emails exchanged _____ us in April.
8. Contracts must be renewed one week _____ their expiration.
9. We will write _____ you as soon as we are _____ a position to supply these goods again.
10. To avoid possible dispute _____ quality, both sides should describe the goods clearly in the contract.

CHAPTER V   ORDERS AND CONTRACTS

III. Translate the following sentences into English.

1. 经过长时间友好的讨论，现达成一笔 50,000 条床单的交易。
2. 我们高兴地确认从你处购进了 300 吨钢板。
3. 请放心，一旦新货源到来，我们立刻重提此事。
4. 如果能降价 5%，我们会考虑再追加一个 40 尺柜的订单。
5. 根据我们昨晚讨论的，麻烦你尽快把修改好的订单发给我。

Lesson 12

Sending S/C and PI

收到订金或者信用证是订单最终确认的依据。客户确认订单之后，仍需要确认订金的到达日期，这样有利于安排生产。正式生产前还需跟客人确认产前样，确认样可以是为了大货做的确认样，也可以是为了销售样等做的确认样，而大货样/船样（shipment sample）是生产结束后，从大货中抽出来的样品，寄给客户看的。

From: Celia
To: Mikhail
Sent: Nov. 22, 2018
Subject: SS10 order (WS002 and WS003)

Dear Mikhail,

Thanks for your order. Please note we sent below separately:

1) Confirmation samples
We will send out 3 pairs of confirmation samples for above styles. These samples will arrive at Xiamen office on September 30. Please advise if you can receive and confirm these samples on that day. We need you confirm these samples before Oct. 1, 2018 (China Time) urgently.

2) S/C and PI
Attached S/C (Sales Contract) and PI (Proforma Invoice) of 09UF-1150 and 09UF-1151 in duplicate. If all is correct, pls sign and stamp and send back S/C#09UF-1150 and 09UF-1151 to us for our file.

Remarks:

We need to purchase materials for above new orders.

Before we purchase materials, we need to receive 20% deposit and S/C signed back as order confirmation.

Best regards,

Celia

1. **in duplicate** 一式两份

    in triplicate/in three copies 一式三份

    in quadruplicate/in four copies 一式四份

    in quintuplicate/in five copies 一式五份

    in sextuplicate/in six copies 一式六份

    in septuplicate/in seven copies 一式七份

    in octuplicate/in eight copies 一式八份

    in nonuplicate/in nine copies 一式九份

    in decuplicate/in ten copies 一式十份

2. **sign** *v.* 手势；签字

    n. 标记；标牌，指示牌；招牌

    In order to validate the agreement, both parties sign it.

    为使协议有效，双方在上面签了字。

3. **stamp** *vt.* 铭记；标出；盖章于……

    The girl forgot to stamp my library book.

    那位姑娘忘了在我借的书上盖借出日期章了。

4. **for our file** 以备查询

    Please sign and return one copy for our file.

    请将本确认书的一份签署后寄还本公司以备查询。

    Please sign and return one copy for our file at your earliest convenience.

    请尽快签退一份，以备我方存查。

CHAPTER V ORDERS AND CONTRACTS

5. purchase materials 采购材料

Any company that wants to purchase materials should obtain loans from banks, repaying them with interest. 任何单位要取得物资，都要从银行贷款，并且付利息。

I. Translate the following expressions into Chinese or vice versa.

1. confirmation samples
2. in duplicate
3. as agreed
4. order confirmation
5. trial order
6. 一式三份
7. 采购材料
8. 以备查询
9. 生产样
10. 签订合同

II. Fill in the appropriate words or expressions listed in the box and put the letter into Chinese.

for your good cooperation	in duplicate	duly countersigned
prove satisfactory	for your file	in the meantime	repeat order	enclosing
in your favor	established with	terms and conditions

Dears Sirs,

Thank you for your letter of March 2 _____ S/C No. 321 _____ one copy of which we have _____ and are returning one copy _____.

_____ we have established the necessary L/C _____. If the first shipment of 80 tons should _____, we would most likely send you _____ for another 50 tons.

We thank you again _____.

Yours sincerely,

×××

III. Translate the following sentences into English.

1. 请尽快盖章回签。
2. 我方很高兴发现贵方用料品质优良。现寄去2500打胶鞋的小额订单以作试购。
3. 我们同意按以下条款售出下列商品。
4. 按你们的要求，我们随函寄去第456号销售确认书正本三份。
5. 如果你们认为没问题，我们希望你们签回销售合同的副本一份备查。

IV. Write a letter ordering the items listed below, specifying quantity, unit price, total amount and terms of payment, shipment, etc.

品名	数量	货号	价格	价格条件
不粘锅	3500	26"	USD121 per set	CFRC3 Chicago
不粘锅	1400	30"	USD164 per set	CFRC3 Chicago

付款方式：即期汇票信用证
装运时间：12月25日之前及时抵达

Business Link

　　合同内容应详细全面，对双方的权利、义务以及发生争执的处理均有详细规定。对大宗商品或成交金额较大的商品交易一般均采用合同形式。由卖方按照双方认可的条款草拟的合同称为销售合同（Sales Contract），由买方草拟的合同称为购货合同（Purchase Contract）。

　　合同的简化形式就是销售确认书（Sales Confirmation）和购货确认书（Purchase Confirmation）。异议、索赔、仲裁、不可抗力等一般条款都不会列入销售确认书或购货确认书。确认书适用成交金额不大、批次较多的轻工日用品、小土特产品，或已有代理等长期协议的交易。不管是合同还是确认书，一般都是一式两份，经过双方签字，各执一份，据以执行，这种行为在进出口业务中，称为签订合同。

外贸合同的基本框架及内容：

1. Title（合同名称及其编号）。
2. Preamble（序文）：包括签约日期、地点以及当事人名称、地址及其法律地位。
3. Name of Commodity（商品名称）。
4. Quality Clause（品质条款）：包括约定品质的决定方式及其时间和地点。
5. Quantity Clause（数量条款）：包括约定数量单位、交付数量的决定时间和地点，

CHAPTER V ORDERS AND CONTRACTS

以及溢短装数量的解决办法等。

6. Price Clause（价格条款）：包括价格种类、结构、使用货币计算单位以及币值或价格变动风险的归宿等。
7. Packing Clause（包装条款）：包括包装的方式、方法、包装的材料以及唛头等。
8. Delivery Clause（交货期）：包括交货时间、地点、交货方式、交货通知等。
9. Payment Clause（支付条款）：包括支付方式、支付工具以及支付时间等。
10. Insurance Clause（保险条款）：包括由何方保险、投保险别、金额与货币约定保险人等。
11. Inspection Clause（检验条款）：包括项目、检验时间与地点、检验机构、检验方法、检验效力及其费用的负担等。
12. Claim Clause（索赔条款）：包括索赔的期限及其通知方法、应提出的证明文件、索赔货物和付款的关系，以及解决索赔的基本原则。
13. Arbitration Clause（仲裁条款）：包括范围、地点、仲裁机构及其费用的负担等。
14. Force Majeure Clause（不可抗力条款）：包括不可抗力事故的原因、通知时间和方法、应提出的文件，以及免责事项等。
15. Breach and Cancellation of Contract Clause（违约及解除契约权条款）：包括违约的处理方法、解约事由和解约后的赔偿等。
16. Miscellaneous Clause（其他条款）：依据契约的性质和具体情况，可以包括进出口许可证。

Business English Correspondence (2nd Edition)
商务英语函电（第二版）

Skill Training

Exercise I. Fill in the blanks according to the following information.

外方： S.W. TRADING CO., LTD.
地址： 283 WATER ROAD, ALPERTON
WEMBLEY, MIDDLESEX HAO 1HX
U.K. ENGLAND

合同号码：UEO-01387

合同日期：JAN. 25, 2021

品名/数量： 1) 草编手袋 (STRAW BAGS)
HB34-065　　　850　DOZEN
HB87-070　　　850　DOZEN

2) 草编拖鞋 (STRAW SANDALS)
T-011　　　337　DOZEN
T-024　　　337　DOZEN

单价：　　　　　　　CIF FELIXSTOWE
HB34-065　　USD14.93/DOZ　　　T-011　　USD16.81/DOZ
HB87-070　　USD15.67/DOZ　　　T-024　　USD14.66/DOZ

包装： 货号HB34-065，HB87-070　每2打装1纸箱；
货号T-011，T-024　每2打装1纸箱；
共3个20尺集装箱。

L/C远期30天付款，2021年2月底前到证，2021年3月底前装运
装运港SHANGHAI，　目的港FELIXSTOWE
不许分批，允许转运
按发票总金额加一成投保 I.C.C.的A险和战争险。

CHAPTER V   ORDERS AND CONTRACTS

SALES CONFIRMATION

S/C No.: _____
Date: _____

The Seller: YONGYE NATIVE PRODUCE IMP. & EXP. CORP.
Address: 18 DIAN CHI ROAD
SHANGHAI 200002
CHINA

The Buyer: S.W. TRADING CO., LTD.
Address: 283 WATER ROAD, ALPERTON
WEMBLEY, MIDDLESEX HAO 1HX
U.K. ENGLAND

Item No.	Commodity & Specifications	Unit	Quantity	Unit Price (US$)	Amount (US$)
1	STRAW BAGS HB34-065 HB87-070				
2	STRAW SANDALS T-011 T-024				

TOTAL CONTRACT VALUE:

PACKING:

TIME OF SHIPMENT:

TERMS OF PAYMENT:

INSURANCE:

Confirmed by:
THE SELLER
YONGYE NATIVE PRODUCE IMP. & EXP. CORP.
MANAGER

(Signature)

THE BUYER

(Signature)

Exercise II. Fill in the Proforma Invoice with the given information.

埃及公司 James Brown & Sons 打算向 ST Trading Co., Ltd. 公司购买 5000 个化妆包（Model No.: A156）。按他们的要求，ST Trading Co., Ltd. 公司于 7 月 22 日为该公司开具了号码为 PI20110407 的形式发票：每个化妆包单价为 USD2.80 FOB Xiamen, 包装：12 units per master carton，付款方式：保兑的、不可撤销的信用证。

Cosmetic Bag

Model No.: A156   Size: 24cm × 16cm × 6cm   Material: Cowherd Material

Issuer:		PROFORMA INVOICE	
To:		No. :	Date:
		Terms of payment:	
Tansport details From Xiamen, China to:		Contract No.:	
Marks and numbers	Number and kind of packages; description of goods	Unit price	Quantity	Amount
N/M	Size: Packing:	FOB Xiamen		
TOTAL:				

Authorized signature:
Insurance:
Time of delivery:
Bank name: AGRICULTURAL BANK OF CHINA, XIAMEN BRANCH KEJIYUAN SUB-BRANCH
Swift: ABOCCNBJ800, A/C NO.: 40352014040003753
Bank address: 1/F HENGSHENG BUILDING, YUEHUA ROAD, HULI DISTRICT, XIAMEN, P.R. CHINA

CHAPTER V　ORDERS AND CONTRACTS

Exercise III. Fill in the contract form with information gathered from the following correspondences.

Mail 1

Hangzhou Deluxe International Ltd.
Address: 14D, 68 Nanjing Road, Hangzhou, China
Tel: 86 571 8573 6501
Fax: 86 571 8573 0275
Website: www.deluxe.com.cn
Email: stever@deluxe.com.cn

July 2, 2018

Claven Stationery S.A.
20 Masquire Place
Paris, France

ATTN: Miss Claudia Venegas

Dear Miss Claudia Venegas,

I'm writing to reintroduce myself as Steven Wang representing Hangzhou Deluxe International Ltd. I'm glad to have met you at the 123rd Canton Fair where you took some interest in our products.

We are a manufacturer and exporter of cork and wooden products, including stationery toys, promotions and Christmas items. Most of our products are exported to American and European markets. Because our factory is located in the Free Trade Zone, we enjoy some favorable policies from the Government. Therefore we can provide more competitive prices than other producers.

I hereby send you some photos of our products for your reference. Should any of them be of interest to you, please let us know.

Best regards,
Steven Wang
Encl. Photos

Mail 2

From: claudia@hotmail.com
To: steven@deluxe.com.cn
Sent: Thursday, July 10, 2018 11: 40 AM

Hello Steven,

Thank you for your letter and photos. We are interested in items DXA3017 and DXA3012.

But we need you to send samples. Our FedEx account is : 19642384-2.

Awaiting your prompt reply.

My best regards,
Claudia Venegas

Mail 3

发件人：steven@deluxe.com.cn
收件人：claudia@hotmail.com
发送时间：2018 年 7 月 11 日 15: 18
主题：cork memo board

Dear Miss Claudia Venegas,

Thank you for your prompt reply.

We have sent the samples to you today. I guess you will receive them in three days.

But we have to mention that the design and wording on them are for one of our previous customers. Please inform us of your own designs on the boards when you send us an order.

Sincerely yours,
Steven Wang

CHAPTER V ORDERS AND CONTRACTS

Mail 4

From: claudia@hotmail.com
To: steven@deluxe.com.cn
Sent: Monday, July 14, 2018 2: 49 PM

Hello Steven,

Once again thanks for your message. Just yesterday we received your samples. Thanks and we will work on the order and get back to you.

My best regards,
Claudia Venegas

Mail 5

发件人：steven@deluxe.com.cn
收件人：claudia@hotmail.com
发送时间：2018 年 7 月 26 日 10: 37
主题：cork memo board

Dear Miss Claudia Venegas,

Good morning!

In your previous email you agreed to work on the order and get back to me, but so far we haven't received your order.

Do you still need these cork memo boards? If so, we can guarantee the best quality and the most competitive prices, because we have our own factory with advanced equipment. We also have a long and stable relationship with cork suppliers, and we can get the best prices from them. So we know how to cut cost without affecting the quality and delivery date.

I'm sure our first deal will be successful!

Sincerely yours,
Steven Wang

Mail 6

From: claudia@hotmail.com
To: steven@deluxe.com.cn
Sent: Sunday, July 27, 2018 2: 09 PM

Hello Steven,

Our designs are ready. We have sent them to you today by courier.

Will you please quote us your best prices for items DXA3017 and DXA3012? We need 1" × 20" container load to begin with.

Please also state your terms of payment.

Please reply ASAP.

Yours,
Claudia Venegas

Mail 7

发件人：steven@deluxe.com.cn
收件人：claudia@hotmail.com
发送时间：2018 年 7 月 27 日 17: 03
主题：cork memo board

Dear Miss Claudia Venegas,

Thank you for your prompt reply. The following is our quotation for the quantity of 1" × 20" container.

    DXA3017: USD4.40/piece FOB Ningbo
    DXA3012: USD4.35/piece FOB Ningbo

Each one with 5 pushpins in yellow, red, green, blue and white respectively, in shrink pack. 20 pieces packed in a double layer corrugated carton (dimensions: 41.5cm × 61.5cm × 33cm).

Payment by sight L/C or T/T. In case of T/T we need 30% deposit before production, 70% upon faxing copy of B/L.

CHAPTER V　ORDERS AND CONTRACTS

I believe the above is acceptable.

Awaiting your favorable reply.

Yours,
Steven Wang

Mail 8

From: claudia@hotmail.com
To: steven@deluxe.com.cn
Sent: Sunday, July 28, 2018 9: 49 AM

Dear Steven,

I confirm your offer of yesterday. The quantities for our order are:
　　　　　　DXA3017: 3,000 pieces
　　　　　　DXA3012: 3,000 pieces

We prefer to pay by T/T and we agree to your T/T terms.

When is your best delivery date?

Please also tell me how many PCS you usually pack per carton and per inner box.

Best regards,
Claudia Venegas

Mail 9

发件人：steven@deluxe.com.cn
收件人：claudia@hotmail.com
发送时间：2018 年 7 月 29 日 11: 53
主题：cork memo board

Dear Claudia,

The prices we offered are for cork memo boards packed in cartons of 20 PCS each, without inner boxes. However, if you insist on inner boxes, they are subject to a cost of 9 cents each.

The following is our T/T remittance routine:

    BANK: Bank of China, Hangzhou Branch
      No. 37 Zhoushan Road, Hangzhou, China
  IN FAVOR OF: Hangzhou Deluxe International Ltd.
  ADDRESS: 14D, 68 Nanjing Road, Hangzhou, China
  A/C NO.: 654123687423145

Our delivery date will be 20 days after we receive your 30% deposit.

Please reply soon, stating the port of destination.

Best regards,
Steven Wang

Mail 10

From: claudia@hotmail.com
To: steven@deluxe.com.cn
Sent: Wednesday, July 30, 2018 10: 41 AM

Hi Steven,

I accept the 9 cents cost for inner boxes.

Our port of destination is Nice.

Please prepare a sales contract for us to sign.

Best regards,
Claudia

注：
1. cork memo board: 软木留言板
2. pushpins: 图钉
3. shrink pack: 吸塑包装

CHAPTER V ORDERS AND CONTRACTS

根据上面的信息填制下面的英文合同。

Sales Contract

No. 2003DX0100
Date: August, 8th, 2018

Sellers:

Hangzhou Deluxe International Ltd.

To: (Buyers)

Claven Stationery S.A. Paris, France

This Sales Contract is made out as per the following terms and conditions confirmed by both parties.

Name of Commodity:					
Specifications or Item No.	PCS per CTN	CTNS	Quantity (PCS)	Unit Price	Amount
Total					
Quantity allowance: ± 5%					
Total Value:					

(Continued)

Time of shipment:

Shipping mark:

Port of loading:

Prot of destination:

Packing:

Payment:

Insurance:

Force majeure: The Seller shall not be held liable for failure or delay in delivery of the entire lot or a portion of the Commodity under this contract in consequence of any force majeure incidents.

Arbitration: Any or all disputes arising from or in connection with the performance of the Contract shall be settled through negotiation by both parties, failing which they shall be submitted for arbitration. The arbitration shall take place in China and shall be conducted by the CIETAC in accordance with the rules of procedures of the said commission. The arbitration award shall be final and binding upon both Buyers and Sellers. Unless otherwise awarded by the said arbitration commission, the arbitration fees shall be borne by the losing party.

Other conditions:

Buyers (Signature)   Sellers (Signature)

Useful Expressions

1. We are pleased to place an order with you for the following items on the understanding that they can be supplied from stock at the prices quoted.
2. Thank you for your quotation of March 5 and the samples of the footwears. We are pleased to place an order with you on the terms stated in your fax.
3. We are sending you our Sales Contract No. 5690 in duplicate. Please countersign and

CHAPTER V ORDERS AND CONTRACTS

return one copy for our file as soon as possible.

4. If the first order is satisfactorily executed, we shall place repeat orders with you.
5. The chief difficulty in accepting your orders now is the heavy backlog of commitments. But you may rest assured that as soon as we are able to accept new orders, we shall give priority or preference to yours.
6. Your order is booked and will be executed with great care. Please open the covering L/C, which must reach here one month before the date of shipment.
7. We have accepted your order No. 35 for 20,000 yards of pongee silk article No. 567. Please send us color assortment immediately and open the relevant L/C according to the terms and conditions agreed upon.
8. Please follow our shipping instructions carefully and make sure that our order is executed to the entire satisfaction of our customers with the least possible delay.
9. It is regrettable to see an order dropped owing to no agreement on price, however, we wish to recommend you another quality at a lower price for your consideration.
10. While thanking you for your order, we have to say that supplies of raw materials are becoming more and more difficult to obtain, and we have no alternative but to decline your order.

CHAPTER VI
PRODUCTION & INSPECTION

Objectives:

After learning this chapter, you will

1. master commonly used expressions of commodity inspection.
2. master the ways to describe commodity inspection.
3. understand the approach to communicate with others on commodity inspection.

Introduction

生产进度跟踪的基本要求是使生产企业能按订单及时交货。及时交货就必须使生产进度与订单交货期相吻合，尽量做到不提前交货，也不延迟交货。外贸业务员接到订单后，需与生产企业或本企业有关负责人对订单内容逐一进行分解，将其转化为企业下达生产任务的生产通知单。如遇意外事件导致订单无法按时按质完成，外贸业务员需要反复核实，并做好多种应急事件处理准备工作，或及时调整生产通知单个别内容，或及时调整生产厂家另行下达生产通知。

外贸业务员通过生产管理部门每日的"生产日报表"统计，调查每天的成品数量及累计完成数量，以了解生产进度并加以跟踪控制，以确保能按订单要求准时交货。外贸业务员发现实际进度与计划进度产生差异，应及时查找原因。如属进度发生延误导致影响交货期，除追究责任外，应要求企业尽快采取各种补救措施，如外包或加班等。补救措施无效，仍无法如期交货时，外贸业务员应及时联络并争取境外客户谅解，并征求延迟交货日期。

商品检验检疫是指对商品的品质、重量、包装、残损以及货物装运技术条件进行检验和鉴定，以确定交货的品质、数量和包装等是否与合同规定一致，并符合国家有关法律、行政法规的规定以及国际惯例等。CCIB是授权检查进出口商品质量，数量及各种其他的检验标准和公证外贸相关单据的机构。

CHAPTER VI   PRODUCTION & INSPECTION

Writing Strategy

1. 提及订单，告知验货的结果。
2. 若有问题，可要求卖方重新检验货物并采取补救措施，加班生产。
3. 若无法按时收货，提出赔偿并要求解释。
4. 期待性结尾。

Lesson 13

(A) Inline Inspection Reports

很多大客户和专业客户，在下了订单以后，一般是要进行验厂的，目的是了解供应商的真实情况。根据生产情况，可以通过生产初期、中期、出货前、出货等不同程序对产品进行检验。验货方式有DUPRO（生产过程中验货）、FRI（最终产品检验）和TRI（按验货协定对全数进行检验）三种方式。在货物生产过程中，也需要跟客户保持互动，让对方知道目前订单的进展。这样一旦有紧急情况，就不至于措手不及。

From: Jazz Xie
To: Celia
CC: 'Alexander'; 'AAzarov'; 'Irina Popelko'
Subject: WS002, WS003-Citishoes-Inline inspection reports

Dear Celia,

I did the inline inspections for Citishoes style WS002 and WS003 today, but the quality for both styles is unacceptable, the defective rate is over 40% for both styles. Please ask your QCs to recheck all the shoes strictly according to the confirmation samples and pay more attention for the cleaning of the uppers during reworking.

More details please kindly refer to the attached inspection reports. Thanks!

Best regards,

Jazz

Footwear Dept. Manager

Footmaster Xiamen Office

+86 592 1234567 (office Xiamen)

+86 592 7654321 (fax Xiamen)

+86 138 12345678 (mobile China)

----

www.sportmaster.ru

(B) Advising the Production Schedule

From: Celia
To: Jazz
Sent: October 10, 2018
Subject: production status

Dear Jazz,

Thank you for your mail.

We followed your inspection guidance and improved our production status.

For new production schedule, please kindly see attached.

We will update production status by "Supplier's Weekly Production Schedule" form each Friday so you can get prompt information.

Note: to meet delivery date and catch vessel, please come to our factory for final inspection on Dec. 18.

Thanks.

Best regards,
Celia
(CC: Mr. Benjamin Chan)

CHAPTER VI   PRODUCTION & INSPECTION

1. **inline inspection** 中期验货

   这是指货物完成一部分所做的检验，比如完成 30% 时验一次，完成 60% 时再验一次，完货后再做"final inspection"（尾期验货）。

   inspection n. 检验

   I think DUPRO (During Production Check) inspection is necessary.

   我觉得产中验货是有必要的。

   Inspection Report 检验报告

   Inspection Certificate 检验证书

   商检证书的种类主要有：

   Inspection Certificate of Quality 质量检验证书

   Inspection Certificate of Quantity 数量检验证书

   Inspection Certificate of Weight 重量检验证书

   Inspection Certificate of Origin 产地检验证书

   Inspection Certificate of Health 健康检验证书

   Inspection Certificate on Damaged Cargo 残损检验证书

   Disinfection Inspection Certificate 消毒检验证书

   值得说明的是，检验证书的签发日期一般早于运输单据的出单日期。

2. **defective** a. 缺陷的，损坏的

   In other words, if the product is not accessible for target users, then the product is defective.

   换句话说，如果产品对目标用户是不可使用的，那么该产品是有缺陷的。

   We tender our humble apologies for these defective parts.

   对于这些损坏的部件，我们深感抱歉。

   While we try our best to avoid any losses, occasionally a defective one escapes our best efforts. 我们尽力去避免损失，但依然百密一疏。

3. **QC: quality controller** 质检员

   相当于一般企业中的产品检验员，包括进货检验员（IQC）、制程检验员（IPQC）和最终检验员（FQC）。但是，平常人们也称他们为跟单员。

4. **guidance** n. 指导

   Your presence and guidance are requested. 敬请莅临指导。

5. **production status** 生产情况

   When each step is completed, the production order reflects this by a change in the production status.
   当每一个步骤完成时,生产订单会反映出生产状态在这一步的变化。

6. **update** *n.* 最新的情况,最新的信息

      v. 更新,为……提供最新信息

   I'll need updates on your progress. 我需要了解你的最新进展情况。

   We are now informing you of the updates on production of Rome curtains.
   兹告知你方罗马窗帘生产进度最新情况。

   We will update you the latest price regarding this model.
   我们会向你提供这种型号最新的价格。

   Pls send me updated offer sheet ASAP. 请马上发我更新过的报价单。

7. **prompt** *a.* 立即的,及时的

   Prompt payment of bills is greatly appreciated. 如蒙即期结账,则不胜感激。

8. **vessel** *n.* 轮船,大船

   类似的还有 steamer, liner 和 tramp

   The carrying vessel will sail for your port in early March.
   承运船只将在3月初驶往你方港口。

   Please fax name and approximate sailing date of vessel on which space is booked.
   请传真告知预订舱位轮船的船名以及大约起航的日期。

   container vessel 集装箱专用船

   liner service 班轮运输

   tramp 不定期航线运输

Exercises

I. Translate the following expressions into Chinese or vice versa.

1. production status
2. confirmation sample
3. defective rate
4. inline inspection
5. quality controller
6. 最终验货
7. 检验证书
8. 更新报价
9. 船只
10. 产地检验证书

CHAPTER VI   PRODUCTION & INSPECTION

II. Choose the correct word to complete each sentence.

(   ) 1. We offer a _____ to customers who buy in bulk.
  A. refund   B. discount   C. delivery

(   ) 2. We ask customers who are not fully satisfied to _____ goods within seven days.
  A. refund   B. discount   C. return

(   ) 3. In order to get a full _____, customers must send back goods in the original packaging.
  A. refund   B. discount   C. return

(   ) 4. Goods will be _____ within 24 hours of your order.
  A. dispatched   B. purchased   C. exchanged

(   ) 5. Goods are kept in our _____ until ready for delivery.
  A. stock   B. storage   C. warehouse

(   ) 6. Products and services offered at a large discount are generally a(n) _____.
  A. sale   B. bargain   C. offer

III. Put the following into English.

1. 所有产品在整个生产过程中得通过五道质量检查关。
2. 在装船前买方会派自己的质量检验人员来你的工厂验货。
3. 我们有自己的验货团队来控制产品品质。
4. 请随时告知我方第 A002 号订单的最新情况。
5. 为了按你方要求完成交货，我们的厂家已经加快了生产速度。

Lesson 14

Failed in Inspection

买方会要求卖方在专业机构对货物进行品质检验。有时一些小问题跟客户解释一下，不会影响销售，需要给客户确认。一旦请第三方验货，相对而言对货物和品质的检验会非常专业，往往能发现一些普通验货员或者工厂质检员不容易发现的问题。

From: Ada
To: David
Sent: October 10, 2018
Subject: inspection

Hi David,

We are shocked to inform you that PO#34610, 34614 & 34613 are rejected in final inspection, due to failed outsole blooming test at ITS.

Our outsole supplier tested themselves and passed.

These are the same outsoles that used in the previous orders, the same supplier, and the same good quality as before.

Pls advise & comment.

Best regards,
Ada
(CC: Mr. Benjamin Chan)

1. **inform** *v.* 告知，通知，报告，提供资料

    We shall inform you of the market situation later. 我们以后向你提供市场信息。

    We wish to inform you that business has been done at USD110 per ton.
    兹告知这笔生意已按每吨一百一十美元成交。

    Please be informed that we have already sent the samples requested.
    兹告知我们已寄所需样品。

2. **due to** 由于

    We are unable to guarantee shipment by the agreed date due to a strike at our factory.
    由于工厂罢工，我们无法保证按约定的日期装船发运。

    The damage to the goods is due to improper packing.
    由于包装不当，造成了货物的损害。

CHAPTER VI PRODUCTION & INSPECTION

3. **Blooming Test for Rubber** 橡胶喷霜
   又叫硫黄喷霜，是鞋及皮革物性检测项目之一。
4. **ITS (Intertek Testing Service)** 天祥检验集团
   ITS 是世界上规模最大的工业与消费产品检验公司之一。

I. Translate the following expressions into Chinese or vice versa.

1. Inspection Certificate of Quality
2. Inspection Certificate of Weight
3. Inspection Certificate of Origin
4. due to
5. liner service
6. 不定期航线运输
7. 集装箱专用船
8. 尾期验货
9. 供应商
10. 优良品质

II. Choose the best answer.

(　　) 1. We admit the quality of your products is superior _____ the goods of Japanese origin.
　　　A. to　　　B. than　　　C. with　　　D. over

(　　) 2. Such growing demand has doubtlessly resulted _____ increased prices.
　　　A. in　　　B. from　　　C. at　　　D. for

(　　) 3. We hope we can close a deal _____ USD50, as this is the best price you can obtain.
　　　A. in　　　B. from　　　C. at　　　D. for

(　　) 4. We will inform you _____ the market situation in Asia.
　　　A. in　　　B. to　　　C. of　　　D. for

(　　) 5. Because of their superior quality, our cashmere coats always _____ in Europe.
　　　A. are sold fast　　　B. sell fast
　　　C. have been sold fast　　　D. be sold fast

(　　) 6. _____ the quality problem, please issue the L/G and ship the goods accordingly.
　　　A. As　　　B. Because　　　C. Since　　　D. Due to

III. Put the following into English.

1. 根据 AQL 等级 II 的要求，我们最终通过了验货。
2. 检验报告证明所交货物未达到样品的标准。
3. 兹附上广东商品检验局签发的检验报告。
4. 请填写好验货申请并回传我方。
5. 由于我们长期的业务关系，我尽力拿这个折扣给你。

Lesson 15

Asking to Release the Shipment

有时货物达到了 AQL 标准，但是还会有一些小问题，验货员无法自己做主，需要给客户确认，询问客户是否同意出货或者是交期延后。如果问题不是太大，没有严重的质量问题，客户又急需这批货则会同意出货。如果同意，买方需要出具出货函（Shipment Release Form），卖方就可以出货。反过来买方会要求卖方提供保函（Letter of Guarantee），保证没有严重的质量问题，否则买方有权索赔。

From: Ada
To: Jack
Sent: October 10, 2018
Subject: inspection

Hi, Jack,

We proceed with the production as per your attached mail instructions—revised the detail based on confirmation sample dated Dec. 17, 2017.

Your QC will reject the goods, due to the difference between production sample and confirmation sample dated Dec. 17, 2017.

We are rushing the goods for you to catch your requested Cargo Cut-off Date and Ship Date Jan. 13, 2018.

Pls confirm to release this shipment due to the upper difference. Or the delivery should be postponed.

CHAPTER VI　PRODUCTION & INSPECTION

> Pls confirm today.
>
> Thank you for your help.
>
> Best regards,
> Ada
> (CC: Mr. Benjamin Chan)

1. **proceed** *vi.* 开始；继续进行；发生；行进

    We're not sure whether we still want to proceed with the sale.
    我们不确定是否还要继续减价促销。
    Our project must proceed at a reasonably quick tempo. Surely one.
    这个计划必须尽快进行，一个月的时间应该够了吧？

2. **based on** 以……为基础，基于

    Their price estimates are based on pure guesswork. 他们的估价完全是猜的。
    Our relationship is based on reciprocal respect. 我们的关系是以互相尊重为基础的。

3. **Cargo Cut-off Date** 截关日

    Ship Date 开船日
    时间顺序是先有 ETD（预计开船日），再有 Cargo Cut-off Date，然后是 Ship Date, 最后是 ETA（预计到达日期）。
    cargo *n.* 运输的货物（尤指船货）
    The cargo ex. S.S. "Pearl" has been inspected and found satisfactory.（可以改为 The goods ex. S.S. "Pearl" has been inspected and found satisfactory.）
    装于珍珠轮上的船货已经检查过，结果令人满意。
    说与装船有关的货物时，可用 cargo，但不如 goods 用得普遍。
    We expected to ship the goods（可用 cargo）next week. 我们预计下周装货。
    如果货物不是由船运输就不能用 cargo。
    We are sending you the goods（不能用 cargo）by air. 我们用航空运输方式给你们发货。

4. **release** *vt./n.* 释放；发布；让与

   This payment will release you from any further obligation to the company.
   付了这笔钱之后，你对公司就再也没有别的债务了。
   Prices blipped a shade higher still following the release of GNP figures.
   国民生产总值的数字公布后价格又上涨了一点。

5. **postpone** *v.* 延期，把……放在次要地位，把……放在后面

   Increasing exports can postpone, but not prevent, this reverse.
   增加出口可以推迟——但无法阻止——这种逆转。
   Better to postpone the shipment than to cancel the contract.
   与其撤约还不如延期装运。

I. Translate the following expressions into Chinese or vice versa.

1. inspection between process
2. production sample
3. Inspection Certificate on Damaged Cargo
4. Authentic Surveyor
5. inspection on cleanliness
6. 交货前检验
7. 标签检查
8. 基于
9. 开船日
10. 出货

II. Answer the questions according to the following Inspection Report.

Inspection Report:

Cargo Name	Plastic Parts
Supplier Name	Guangdong Hongjin Plastic Products Co., Ltd.
Order No.	QR1304
Batch No.	AP123
Date of Inspection	2018-10-24
Location of Inspection	Yantian
Contact Person	Alan Liu
Total Weight	2,000KGS
Total Quantity (# of bags/drums)	8,000 PCS

CHAPTER VI PRODUCTION & INSPECTION

(Continued)

Vessel/Voyage	MSC ALEXANDRA - S1048R
BL#	177DWUWUXA4801X
ETD	2018-11-24

Questions:
1. What are the commodities?
2. When is the date of inspection?
3. When will the goods be inspected?
4. When will the goods be completed?
5. What is the vessel's name?

III. Put the following into English.
1. 请告诉我截关日、预计装运日和预计到港日。
2. 货昨天已经出运，预计到港日是1月25日。
3. 麻烦你让货代安排另一班快船。
4. 商品检验工作在到货后一个月内完成。
5. 我们要检查一下这批瓷器是否有破损。

Business Link

关于商品检验，我们一般只需要清楚了解五个方面：买方的检验权、检验的时间和地点、检验机构、检验证书和检验条款。

1. The inspection right for the buyer 买方的检验权

   If the buyer accept the goods without inspection, the buyer can not reject the goods even the buyer found out some problems about the goods later.
   若买方没有利用合理的机会检验货物，那他就放弃了检验货物的权利，也丧失了拒收货物的权利。

2. Place and Time of Inspection 检验的时间和地点

   1) Inspection in Export Country 出口国检验
      (1) inspection at the seller's factory
         在产地检验

(2) shipping quality, weight or quantity as final

装运前或装运时在装运港或装运地检验离岸质量、重量（否定了买方的复验权）

2) Inspection in Import Country 进口国检验

(1) landing quality, weight or quantity as final

在目的港或目的地卸货后检验到岸质量、重量或数量

(2) to make inspection at the user's residence 在最终用户所在地检验

3) Inspection in Export Country and Re-inspection in Import Country

出口国检验、进口国复验

(1) 装运检验证书是卖方要求买方支付货款或要求银行议付时递交的单据之一。

(2) 卸货后的复验证书是买方向卖方提出异议或索赔的依据。

4) Weight Inspection in Export Country and Quality Inspection in Import Country

离岸重量，到岸品质

3. Inspection Authority 检验机构，分为以下几种：

Governmental 官方的检验机构只对特定商品（粮食、药物等）进行检验，如我国的国家市场监督管理总局、美国食品药品监督管理局（FDA）。

Semi-governmental 半官方的检验机构，例如美国保险人实验室（UL）。

Non-governmental 民间机构。国际贸易中的商品检验主要由民间机构承担，民间商检机构具有公证机构的法律地位。比较著名的有：瑞士日内瓦通用鉴定公司（SGS）、英国劳埃氏公证行（Lloyd's Surveyor）、法国船级社（BV）等。

4. Inspection Certificate 检验证书

商检证书的种类主要有：

Inspection Certificate of Quality 质量检验证书

Inspection Certificate of Quantity 数量检验证书

Inspection Certificate of Weight 重量检验证书

Inspection Certificate of Origin 产地检验证书

Inspection Certificate of Health 健康检验证书

Inspection Certificate on Damaged Cargo 残损检验证书

Disinfection Inspection Certificate 消毒检验证书

5. Inspection Clause in Contract 检验条款

检验条款一般包括以下内容：有关检验权的规定、检验或复验的时间和地点、检验机构、检验项目和检验证书、检验标准等。例如：

The certificate of Quality and Weight issued by ××× at the port/place of...shall be part of the documents to be presented for negotiation under the relevant L/C. The claim, if any, shall be lodged within...days after arrival of the goods at the port of destination.

CHAPTER VI PRODUCTION & INSPECTION

Skill Training

提货单是承运人向收货人签发的文件，用于从货运站经营者处提取货品。出货放行单（Shipment Release Form）是检验机构或者客户开给供应商的邮件或者通知，或者是买方指定的质量检测机构签署的"货运许可证"。根据如下订单填写出货放行单。

Purchase Order					
Buyer: ALABRA SUB TRADING EST. 94017 REGALBUTO CATANIA, ITALY	Supplier: FUJIAN ORIENTAL FOOTWEAR IMP. & EXP. CO., LTD. Add: 9/F MINFA BUILDING NO. 88, DONGSHUI ROAD, FUZHOU, CHINA Tel: 86-591-3456789 Mobile: 86-12345678900				
Shipping No.: 03.05.GB24 Port of Departure: Fuzhou Country of Origin: China Conditions: FOB FUZHOU	Latest ETD: 30 Dec. 2018 Payment: L/C at sight Country of Destination: ITALY Port of Arrival: CATANIA Forwarding Agent: OOCL				
	Currency: USD	For assortments and confirmation and production samples: See Page 2			
ORD	ART	NAME	CARTONS	PAIRS	AMOUNT
00024	FAIL	FAIL	3,000	72,000	$48,240.00
00025	FAIL	FAIL	200	4,800	$3,264.00
00026	FAIL	FAIL	300	7,200	$4,608.00
00027	FAIL	FAIL	300	7,200	$4,608.00
00028	FAIL	FAIL	1,500	36,000	$25,200.00
Important: This order is not valid until the confirmation. Samples are confirmed in writing and signed by Fujian Oriental Footwear Imp. & Exp. Co., Ltd. By acceptance of our order the supplier is unconditionally committed to deliver our orders in accordance with our purchase and other details in our order sheets. Supplier needs to supply to the buyer an official report which proofs that the goods are free of AZO, Cadmium, Nickel, PCB etc. This report is required by European Law.					

SHIPMENT RELEASE FORM (SAMPLE)

DATE :	
CUSTOMER :	
VENDOR:	
MERCHANDISE :	

P.O. NUMBER （订单号）	STYLE NUMBER （款号）	QUANTITY （数量）	CARTON QTY （箱数）

—THE ABOVE ORDERS CAN BE SENT TO OUR FREIGHT FORWARDERS FOR SHIPMENT.

以上订单之商品，可送往货运公司付运。

—IN THE EVENT OF ANY CLAIM ON THESE GOODS, YOU AGREE THAT YOUR COMPANY WILL BE HELD FULLY RESPONSIBLE.

若客人对付运之商品有任何索偿，供货商均需承担所有责任及赔偿。

—THIS FORM WITH A DULY AUTHORIZED SIGNATURE OF REDCATS ASIA IS REQUIRED TO ACCOMPANY THE MERCHANDISE WHEN DELIVERED TO CUSTOMER'S DESIGNATED FORWARDER. THE FORWARDER SHOULD REJECT ANY SHIPMENTS WITHOUT THE REDCATS SHIPMENT RELEASE FORM.

货品付运时，供货商必须连同本公司已签署之货运许可证交付货运公司，否则货运公司可拒绝安排付运上述之商品。

Name of SUB TRADING EST. Representative （代办人）：_____

Signature （代办人签署）：_____

CHAPTER VI　PRODUCTION & INSPECTION

Name of Seller/Factory/Company（供货商名称）：_____

Signature of Seller（供货商签署）：_____

Useful Expressions

1. If your requested inspection date is on Wednesday to Friday, ABC will provide you the inspector name and mobile phone number by fax before 5: 00 pm on the previous Monday.
2. Inspection request form MUST be submitted at least 7 working days prior to the request inspection date.
3. We'll accept the goods only if the results from the two inspections are identical with each other.
4. What if the results from the inspection and the reinspection do not coincide with each other?
5. Our certificates are made valid by means of the official seal and personal chop of the commissioner.
6. As a rule, our certificate is made out in Chinese and English.
7. If the buyer accepts the goods without inspection, the buyer can not reject the goods even the buyer found out some problems about the goods later.
8. The Certificate of Quality and Weight issued by ×׈ at the port/place of...shall be part of the documents to be presented for negotiation under the relevant L/C. The claim, if any, shall be lodged within...days after arrival of the goods at the port of destination.
9. On the strength of the CCIB'S survey report, we hereby lodge a claim against you for US$650.

CHAPTER VII
PAYMENT

Objectives:

After learning this chapter, you will

1. be acquainted with all types of international trade settlement.
2. understand the applications of different modes of payment in international trade.
3. master typical sentences and expressions in writing the letters on terms of payment.
4. be able to write reply letters concerning the above.

Introduction

付款方式也是影响订单的因素之一。国际贸易的付款方式主要分为三种，即汇付（Remittance）、托收（Collection）和信用证（Letter of Credit）。常用的有两种，一种是汇付中的电汇，另一种是信用证。

汇付即通过进、出口商双方所在地银行的汇兑业务进行结算，主要有电汇（T/T）、信汇（M/T）和票汇（D/D）三种方式。无论采用哪种方法，货运单据都是由出口商自行寄给进口商，银行并不经手，所以汇付又称为单纯支付。电汇T/T又可以分为前T/T和后T/T。前T/T就是合同签订后，先付一部分订金，一般都是30%，生产完毕，通知付款，付清余款，然后发货，交付全套单证。不过前T/T比较少见一点，在欧美国家出现得比较多。因为欧美国家的客户处在信誉很好的环境，所以也就非常信任别人。最为多见的是后T/T，收到订金，安排生产，出货，客户收到单证后，付余款；卖家收到余款后，寄送全套单证。T/T订金的比率，是谈判和签订合同的重要内容。订金的比率最低应该是够你把货发出去和拖回来。万一客户拒付，也就没有多大损失。

信用证是银行应进口商请求开给出口商的一种保证付款的凭证，是目前国际贸易付款方式最常用的一种付款方式。由于银行保证付款，对买卖双方都有保障，银行信用代替了商业信用，所以相对安全可靠。但是由于操作比较复杂，手续费用高，与T/T比较各有优缺点。所以在实际操作中，与T/T结合起来，就相当保险，30% T/T，70% balance L/C。

CHAPTER VII PAYMENT

　　托收是出口商根据外贸合同规定，将货物装运出口后，开立以进口方为付款人的商业汇票并附上有关单据，委托当地银行通过进口商所在地银行向进口商代收货款后，汇回出口商的一种结算方式。托收分为光票托收（不附带任何货运单据的汇票或附有"非货运单据"：垫款清单/商检证明）和跟单托收。跟单托收又主要涉及付款交单（D/P）和承兑交单（D/A）两种方式。承兑交单（Documents against Acceptance）是在跟单托收方式下，出口方（或代收银行）向进口方以承兑为条件交付单据的一种办法。承兑交单的方式使出口商处于较大风险而鲜少被采用，因为该方式规定进口商只要承兑汇票就可得到货运单据。D/P风险很大，但是如果和T/T结合起来，也不失为一种非常好的交货方式。有些国家的一些公司喜欢用D/P，可以采用30% T/T in advance, 40% after shipment, the balance D/P, 这种方式比后T/T还要保险。

　　鉴于目前激烈的贸易竞争和互联网的兴盛，很多涉及小额交易的电子商务基本采用快递业务避税，即其付款相应地采用开通国际支付功能的个人支付卡，如PayPal（贝宝），Western Union（西联汇款），MoneyGram（速汇金）。

Writing Strategy

　　1. 首先要熟悉各种付款方式的优点和缺点，以及哪一种付款方式对己方最有利。一般来说，对于信誉比较好的客户可以适当给予较为宽松的付款方式。

　　2. 书写要求更为宽松的付款方式的信函时，应首先指出相关订单或合同，然后提出具体的付款要求并说明原因，最后希望对方接受。书写要求更改付款方式的信函还要进一步指出原来的付款方式及要求更改的原因。

　　3. 对于上述信函的回复首先要说明收到对方的来信，然后表明你是接受还是拒绝并说明原因。如果拒绝，但做出一些让步需具体说明。注意做出让步时不应太干脆，以免让对方认为还有进一步让步的可能。

　　4. 对于催促结款信函，应具体说明总额、已付款额、尾款余额，并具体准确地提供银行账户。

Lesson 16

Payment Negotiation

　　付款方式与商品的价格紧密联系。付款及时，商品价格也会优惠，所以国际贸易中的讨价还价并不仅仅是价格，对付款方式的磋商也是还盘中的一个环节。信誉好的大公司一般可以得到优惠的付款方式。客户采取远期付款，对于客户的融资有利。因为客户在一定时间内，可能已经卖完所有产品，货款已经进账，等于是利用出口商的钱去赚钱。但对于出口商来说，资金被占用太久，不利于内部周转，但有利于增加业务量。

From: Ada
To: David
Subject: payment terms

Hi David,

Thank you for your mail today.

We will try to work with our Finance Dept.

Concerning our cash flow, we can only accept 30 days payment terms. But we confirm offering 60 days terms to Walmart only.

If the payment terms goes beyond attached listed, we will have problem in cash flow. Therefore we cannot accept orders for customers who request more than 60 days.

For customers who can meet our payment terms, we shall offer best price.

Thank you for your cooperation.

Best regards,
Ada
(CC: Mr. Benjamin Chan)

1. **payment** *n.* （不可数）支付；（可数）支付的款
   terms of payment 或 payment terms 支付条款
   payment on deferred terms 远期（延期）付款

CHAPTER VII   PAYMENT

monthly payment of RMB ￥30,000 每月付人民币三千元

1) 付某种费用的款，如发票、费用、佣金等，常用"in payment of"。
We are enclosing our Cheque No. B123 issued by the Barclays' Bank, London for Stg. £2000 in payment of your Invoice No. 56.
兹寄去伦敦巴克莱银行所开的第 B123 号支票一张，金额计 2000 英镑，系付你方的 56 号发票之款。

2) 付某种具体事物的款，如商品、广告、样品等，常用"in payment for"。
We airmailed you yesterday a series of "Hua Sheng" Brand Electric Fans as samples and looking forward to your USD230 in payment for the above.
我方昨日空邮去"华生"牌电扇系列样品，并盼望收到你方金额计 230 美元的支票，以偿付上述样品。

pay *vt.* 付（款项，费用等）；给予（主意等）；进行（访问等）
   vi. 付款；值得；合算

pay in advance 预付

pay by installments 分期付款

pay on delivery 货到付款

pay for *ph.v.* 付出代价，为了得到……而付款

payable *adj.* 可付的，应付的

bills payable 应付票据

a cheque payable at sight 见票即付的支票

amount payable 应付金额

2. 60 days terms 六十天支付的付款方式，指远期付款方式

60 days' D/P 六十天期付款交单

以见票三十天议付的信用证为例，介绍下面几种常见的说法：

L/C available by draft at 30 days after sight;

(usance/time/term) L/C at 30 days after sight;

(usance/time/term) at 30 days;

30 days (usance/time/term) L/C.

time L/C; term L/C; usance L/C 远期信用证

3. cash flow 资金流动；现金流动量

Operating cash flow last year totaled 17.8 billion yuan.
去年经营现金流总计人民币 178 亿元。

4. Walmart 沃尔玛百货有限公司
沃尔玛百货有限公司是一家美国的世界性连锁企业，连续 7 年在美国《财富》杂志世界 500 强企业中居首位。沃尔玛公司有 8500 家门店，分布于全球 15 个国家。

5. meet *v.* 满足，支付

meet one's account = to pay 支付款项

We are sure they will meet the draft on presentation.

我们肯定他们在汇票交付时即予付款。

Exercises

I. Translate the following expressions into Chinese or vice versa.

1. cash flow
2. payment terms
3. Finance Dept.
4. T/T
5. M/T
6. 票汇
7. 汇付
8. 托收
9. 远期信用证
10. 满足付款条件

II. Decide whether the following statements are true or false. Then write T for true and F for false in the brackets before each statement.

1. If the payment is to be made "30 days' sight", it means that the payment will have to be made 30 days after the issuing of this draft. (　　)
2. So far, documentary credits are the most ideal method of payment to provide security for both buyers and sellers. Therefore, in whatever conditions, L/C should be the first consideration in the method of payment for transactions. (　　)
3. The negotiating bank is usually referring to the issuing bank in the importing country. (　　)
4. To the seller, payment by D/P is much safer than by D/A. (　　)
5. On the basis of collection, the exporter usually demands the payment first before making shipment so as to protect his interest. (　　)
6. Whoever holds the bill of exchange, he has the right to demand the payment. (　　)

CHAPTER VII PAYMENT

III. Complete the following in English.

1) For this purchase we propose
   a. 以九十天的远期信用证付款。
   b. 以远期信用证付款。
   c. 以英镑付款。

2) As agreed, we have
   a. 航空寄出我方样品。
   b. 已收到贵方关于订单号 PO#123 的余款。
   c. 电汇全部货款。

Lesson 17

(A) Proposing Payment by D/P at Sight

外贸业务常用的付款方式是信用证或要求对方先付一部分订金。但是对于小额订单或关系良好的客户，进口商会要求选择更宽松的付款方式，比如付款交单或 45 天放账（O/A 45 days）。小额样品费还可以通过电子商务平台如 PayPal/Western Union/MoneyGram 来支付。

From: Josef

To: Winnie

Subject: payment for 5 pairs additional samples for FW 2007

Dear Winnie,

We would like to change the payment from L/C to D/P at sight or wire transfer PayPal/Western Union for 5 pairs of additional samples, as it will cost us a great deal when handling L/C for such a small order.

Also pls let me know how many handles will fit into a 20ft container. Please advise your opinion.

Best regards,
Josef/Eva

(B) A Reply to the Above

From: Winnie
To: Josef
Subject: D/P documents requirement for 5 pairs additional samples for FW 2018

Dear Josef/Eva,

As per your requirement, for 5 pairs of additional samples, you would like to change the payment from L/C to D/P at sight. Considering our long-standing friendly relations, we will exceptionally accept payment on D/P at sight basis for this order. We will draw on you a draft at sight through our bank on collection basis. We hope this accommodation will be conducive to our future business.

Kindly provide us D/P instruction details, such as the process, documents you required, etc., so we can follow your instructions, and prepare related documents.

Thank you in advance.

Best regards,
Winnie
(CC: Mr. Danny Chan)

1. **O/A(Open Account Trade)** 赊销，放账。指没有正式单据证明的展期信用。
   O/A 45 days 即买方收到货物内，45 天内付款。
2. **wire transfer** *v.* 银行电汇（美国说法），以电传（telex）、银行间金融电讯网络（swift）方式转账，相当于 T/T。
   You may wire transfer your payment to us. 你可把钱电汇过来。
3. **PayPal** 贝宝
   1998 年 12 月成立，是一家总部在美国的在线支付服务商，允许在使用电子邮件

CHAPTER VII   PAYMENT

来标识身份的用户之间转移资金，避免了传统的邮寄支票或者汇款的方法。

Western Union 西联汇款

西联汇款是世界上领先的特快汇款公司，迄今已有一百多年的历史，是美国财富五百强之一的第一数据公司（FDC）的子公司。

MoneyGram 速汇金

速汇金业务是一种个人间的环球快速汇款业务，可在十几分钟内完成由汇款人到收款人的汇款过程，具有快捷便利的特点。

4. **D/P (Documents against Payment)** 付款交单

   D/P at sight 即期付款交单

   D/P at 30 days sight 30 天期付款交单

   D/A (Documents against Acceptance) 承兑交单

5. **exceptionally** *adv.* 例外地，异常地，特殊地

   For friendship's sake, we may exceptionally consider reducing our price a little, but never to that extent. 为了友谊，我们可以破例将价格降低一点，但绝不会降那么多。

   Central banks reacted quickly with exceptionally large interest rate cuts .

   各国的中央银行做出了迅速的反应，大幅降低了利率。

   exception *n.* 例外，异常，特殊

   As requested, we will make an exception to our rules and accept delivery against 30 days L/C, but this should not be regarded as a precedent.

   按照你方的要求，我们将对我们的惯例破一次例，接受以三十天期信用证办理交货，但不能作为先例。

6. **draw on sb. (for sth.)** 开出汇票向某人收款

   You can draw on us at three months' sight.

   你方可开出见票三个月付款的汇票向我们收款。

   As agreed, we are drawing (a draft) on you for the value of this sample shipment.

   按照商定，对这批货的价款我们开出汇票向你方索取。

   drawings *n.* 用汇票支取的金额

   Your letter of credit is allowed 5% more or less in drawings.

   你方信用证应准许在收款时有 5% 的上下幅度。

   drawer *n.* 出票人，发票人

   drawee *n.* 受票人，（汇票）付款人

7. **on collection basis** 以托收方式

8. **be conducive to** （常与 to 连用）有助于……的；有益于……的

   We believe personal contact will be conducive to the promotion of better understanding.

   我们相信个人的接触将有助于促进更好的了解。

conduce *v.* 有助于（后接 to）

Investigations will conduce to a better analysis of the business situation.

调查将有助于更好地分析交易情况。

9. accommodation *n.* 照顾；通融

We extend to you this accommodation in view of our friendly relations.

鉴于我们的友好关系，我们给你方此次照顾。

accommodate *v.* 照顾；通融

We hope you will accommodate us by allowing 3% commission.

我们希望你方能允许给我们 3% 的佣金。

accommodating *adj.* 照顾的；通融的

We hope you will be accommodating enough to grant our request.

我们希望你方能通融一下，答应我们的要求。

10. instruction *n.* 指示，嘱咐

We are awaiting your payment instructions. 我们期待着你方的付款指示。

Collection Instruction Letter 托收指示函

writing instruction 书面指示

field instruction version 现场验货指导文件

instruct *v.* 通知

Pls instruct your bank to increase the amount of your L/C by £50,000.

请通知你方银行将信用证金额提升至 50,000 英镑。

I. Translate the following expressions into Chinese or vice versa.

1. D/P at sight
2. O/A 45 days
3. drawer
4. wire transfer
5. collection instruction letter
6. 相关单据
7. 40 寸集装箱
8. 以托收的方式
9. 保兑信用证
10. 向……开立汇票

CHAPTER VII　　PAYMENT

II. Translate the following letter into Chinese.

> Dear sirs,
>
> We note from your letter of August 1st that you wish to have a change in payment terms.
>
> Actually there is nothing unusual in our original arrangement. Counting from the time you open credit till the time shipment reach your port, the intervals, which is quite normal, is only about three months. Besides, your L/C is opened when the goods are ready for shipment. In this case, we are sorry that we can not meet your wishes.
>
> As we must insist on our customary practice, we sincerely hope that you will not think us unaccommodating.
>
> Yours faithfully,
> ×××

III. Compose a letter according to the following.

　　福建陶瓷进出口公司（Fujian Ceramics Import & Export Corporation）收到美国艾莉森贸易公司（Erickson Trading Co., Ltd.）要求使用更宽松的付款方式的信。请草拟一封回函，内容包括：

1. 收到贵公司 8 月 7 日来函讨论陶瓷产品交易付款方式。
2. 很遗憾，我方不能接受你方提出的承兑交单的支付方式。
3. 在支付方面，我们只接受保兑的、不可撤销的即期信用证。
4. 考虑到双方友好的贸易关系，我们准备破例接受 60 天期远期信用证的付款方式。
5. 希望贵公司能接受我们的建议并速回复。

Lesson 18

Settling Balance Payment

不管是信用证付款还是 T/T 付款，出货前都要向客户了解并核实出货的细节要求，因为这关系到客户在当地是否可以出关。出货后需要及时提交相关的单据给客户并催款，单据提交一份给银行，也要提交一份给客户，并告知货已经出运。

From: Ada
To: Becky
Subject: balance payment

Hi Becky,

All the goods you ordered were shipped. Attached pls find the CI, PL and copy of B/L.

Pls find below about the payment details:

PO#	30% deposit	70% balance
47839/47846/47847/47848	$6,148.80	$14,347.20
49855/49856/49857	$5,127.30	$11,963.70
Total	$11,276.10	$26,310.90

Kindly arrange the balance payment $26,310.90 to our below account:

* BENEFICIARY NAME: TAIZIN COMPANY LIMITED.
* BENEFICIARY BANK A/C NO.:   004-2-600000
* BENEFICIARY BANK INFORMATION: HSBC, NORTH POINT BRANCH
                                 NO. 306-316 KING'S ROAD,
                                 NORTH POINT, HONG KONG
*SWIFT CODE: HSBC HK HHHKH

Best regards,
Ada

(CC: Mr. Benjamin Chan)

CHAPTER VII PAYMENT

1. **CI=commercial invoice** 出货之前要做的商业发票
   PL=packing list 出货之前要做的装箱单
2. **deposit** *n.* 储蓄，存款；保证金，订金；寄存，寄存品
              v. 储蓄；寄存；付保证金
   A £50 deposit is required when ordering, and the balance is due upon delivery.
   订货时需要交 50 英镑的订金，货到后余款结清。
   Deposit insurance is the way to eliminate the possibility.
   存款保险是消除这种可能性的一种方法。
   Would you please deposit some money with us? 请先交一些保证金给我们好吗？
   The minimum deposit is 1.3 million US dollars.
   这项服务的最低存款要求为 130 万美元。
3. **balance** *n.* 账户余额，尾款
              vt. 结平（账目）
   Could you tell me my account balance? 你能告诉我账户余额吗？
   They were due to pay the balance on delivery. 他们应该在货到时支付余额。
   balance the books 结平账目
4. **beneficiary** *n.* 受益人
   applicant *n.* 申请开证人

I. Translate the following expressions into Chinese or vice versa.

1. deposit
2. balance
3. bank A/C
4. beneficiary
5. settle one's account
6. 结平账目
7. 汇丰银行
8. 银行国际代码
9. 支付余额
10. 存款保险

II. Choose the appropriate words in the brackets.

1. If the amount _____ (exceeded, exceeds) that figure, _____ (an, a) L/C is required.
2. For future transactions D/P will be accepted only if the amount _____ (involved, involving) is not up to USD2,000.
3. After shipment we shall draw on you _____ (for, with, against) the expenses we have paid as per your instructions.
4. For this transaction, we suggest payment _____ (by, in, for) D/P at sight.
5. _____ (Owing to, In spite of) the delay, the ABC company has suffered a loss of USD10,000.

III. Translate the following sentences into English.

1. 付完款后，请通知我们。
2. 买方建议用承兑交单的付款方式。但卖方不愿例外。
3. 我们认为在装运时以电汇方式支付是这笔交易唯一可行的办法。
4. 你方所买的一批样货，按照商定办法，我们将开出即期汇票向你方索款。
5. 我方订单789号的金额没有超过一千英镑，请同意以D/P方式支付，因开立信用证会给我们带来许多花费。

CHAPTER VII   PAYMENT

Skill Training

Exercise I. Fill in the draft according to the L/C.

信用证条款

Opening Bank :	CITIBANK N.A.
L/C No. & Date:	180-4367, 18-08-10
L/C Amount:	USD3,487.50
Applicant:	MAURICIO DEPORTS INTERNATIONAL S.A. PANAMA 1 P.R.
Beneficiary:	APOLLO ENTERPRISE CO., LTD. SHANGHAI, P.R. CHINA
Advising Bank:	CITI Bank of SHANGHAI, CHINA
Draft Term:	CREDIT AVAILABLE WITH ANY BANK IN CHINA BY BENEFICIARY'S DRAFT(S) AT SIGHT ON US
Covering Goods:	500 CARTONS WOODEN TOYS ART. NO. MW5010, MV5390
Date of Draft:	2018-09-15

汇票
Draft (Bill of Exchange)

凭　　　　　　　　　　　　　信用证或购买证第　　　　号
Drawn under　　　　　　　　L/C or No. _____

日期　　　　　　　　按息　　付款
Dated _____ Payable with interest @ _____ % per annum

号码　　汇票金额　　　　　中国　　　年　月　日
No. _____ Exchange for _____ 20_____

见票　　　　　日后（本汇票之副本未付）付
At _____ sight of this FIRST of Exchange (Second of Exchange being paid)

Pay to the order of _____ 或其指定人

金额 _____

The sum of _____

此致
TO _____

129

Exercise II.

场 景

你公司 SHANGHAI HUACHENG IMPORT & EXPORT CORP. [258 YISHAN ROAD, SHANGHAI CHINA TEL: (86 21) 64664491 EMAIL: YYAA@H&C.COM]经过磋商，与韩国的 MYUNG-IL HOUSEHOLD CO. [927-3 WEOLAM-DONG, DALSEO-GU, DAEGU, TAEGU-KWANGYEOKSHI, KOREA 704320 TEL: (82 53) 5823911 FAX: (82 53) 5823915]达成了一笔进口交易，主要成交条件如下：

品名：Bandi Tea Pot and Bug
货号：JY788
价格：USD 21.82 per set CFR Shanghai
数量：12,000 套
包装：10 sets/CTN
装运：9 月 30 日前等量分两批在 INCHON 装运
付款：延期付款信用证，单据到达开证行后三十天付款

昨天，双方签订了购货合同确认书 No. SN05SK，现请你据此填写一份信用证申请书。

其他资料：

开证行：中国人民银行上海分行
数量证明一式三份
制造商签署的质量证明书一式二份
受益人证明的副本在装船通知发出后 48 小时发送给开证申请人

CHAPTER VII PAYMENT

IRREVOCABLE DOCUMENTARY CREDIT APPLICATION

TO: **BANK OF CHINA, SHANGHAI BRANCH**

Applicant (full name and **Email Address**)	Beneficiary (full name and **Email Address**)

Advising Bank	L/C NO.
	Date and place of expiry of the credit

Partial shipments	Transhipment	Amount (both in figures and words)
[ ] allowed [ ] not allowed	[ ] allowed [ ] not allowed	

Loading on board/ dispatch/ taking in charge at / from

SHIPMENT is made not later than

for transportation to

Description of goods:

Bandi Tea Pot and Bug as per S/C NO. SN05SK

Packing:

Credit available with   ANY BANK
[ ] by sight payment   [ ] by acceptance   [ ] by negotiation
[ ] by deferred payment at   30 DAYS AFTER B/L DATE
against the documents detailed herein
[ ] and beneficiary's draft for   % of the inoice value
at
on   OPENING BANK
[ ] FOB   [ ] CFR   [ ] CIF
[ ] or other terms

Documents requied (marked with x):
1. ( ) Signed Commercial Invoice in   copies indicating L/C No. And Contract No.
2. ( ) Full set of   clean on board ocean Bills of lading made out to   THE ORDER
        endorsed   IN BLANK   marked "freight ( ) to collect / ( ) prepaid"
        and showing   FREIGHT AMOUNT   notifying _ APLICANT
3. ( ) Air Waybills showing "freight [ ] to collect/[ ] prepaid [ ] indicating freight amount' and consigned to
4. ( ) Cargo Receipt issued by   consigned to
5. ( ) Insurance Policy / Certificate in   copis, blank endorsed for   % of the invoice value showing claims payable
        at   in the currency of the drafts.
        covering
6. ( ) Packing List / Weight Memo in   copies indicating quantity/gross and net weight of each package and packing conditiions as
        called for by the L/C
7. ( ) Certificate of Quantity/Weight in   copies issued by an independent surveyor at the loading port, indicating the actual surveyed
        quantity/weight of shipped goods as well as the packing condition.
8. ( ) Certificate of Quality in   copies issed by [   ]manufacturer/[   ]public recognized surveyor/ [   ]
9. ( ) Beneficiary's certified copy of cable/telex dispatched to the accountees within   hours after shipment advising [   ]name of
        vessel/ [   ] flight No./ [   ] wagon No, date, quantity, weight and value of shipment
10. ( ) Beneficiary's Certificate certifying that extra copies of the documents have been dispatched according to the contract terms
11. ( ) Shipping Co's Certificate atesting that the carrying vessel is chartered or booked by accountee or their shipping agents:
12. ( ) Other documents, if any:

Additional instuctions:
1. ( ) All banking charges outside the opening bank are for beneficiary's account.
2. ( ) Documents must be presented within   21 days after the date of issuance of the transport documents but within the valicity of
        this credit.
3. ( ) Third party as shipper is not acceptable. Short Form / Blank Back B/L is not acceptable.
4. ( ) Both quantity and amount   % more or less are allowed.
5. ( ) Prepaid freight drawn in excess of L/C amount is acceptable against presentation of original charges voucher issued by shipping Co.
6. ( ) All documents to be forwared in one cover, unless otherwise stated above.
7. ( ) Other terms, if any:

Account No.:   with BANK OF CHINA, SHANGHAI BRANCH   (name of bank)

Transacted by: (Applicant: name, signature of authorized person)

EMAIL: YYAA@H&C.COM

Useful Expressions

1. To develop our business, it is essential to adopt more flexible mode of payment.
2. In view of the small amount of the transaction, we are prepared to accept payment by D/P at sight for the goods shipped.
3. As a special accommodation, we will accept time L/C at 30 days. But I must stress that it relates to this transaction only. We can not regard it as a precedent for future transactions.
4. We regret that we are unable to consider your request for payment under D/A terms.
5. Our usual payment terms are by confirmed irrevocable letter of credit available by draft at sight, accompanied by shipping documents which are to be presented to the negotiating bank at the port of loading.
6. Since both of the contracts are less than 10,000 in value, we would like you to accept D/P as the term of payment.
7. In consideration of our long standing business relationship, we have decided to agree to your suggestion.
8. In the event of our acceptance of your offer, we shall issue a confirmed and irrevocable L/C in your favor.
9. As agreed, the terms of payment for the above orders are letter of credit at 60 days' sight or D/P sight draft.
10. We regret having to inform you that although it is our desire to pave the way for a smooth development of business between us, we cannot accept D/A.
11. Payment is to be made against sight draft drawn under a confirmed, irrevocable, divisible and transferable L/C without recourse for the full amount of purchase.
12. We wish to draw your attention to the fact that as a special sign of encouragement, we shall consider accepting payment by D/P during this sales-pushing stage. We trust this will greatly facilitate your efforts in sales, and we await your favorable reply.
13. The request for easier payment terms is compelled by our funds being tied up in numerous commitments.
14. In order to pave the way for your pushing the sale for our products in your market, we agree to payment for this transaction on D/P terms as a special accommodation.
15. It is expensive to open an L/C and ties up the capital of a small company like ours. So it's better for us to adopt D/P or D/A.

CHAPTER VIII
ESTABLISHMENT OF L/C AND AMENDMENT TO L/C

Objectives:

After learning this chapter, you will

1. be acquainted with the characteristics of the letter of credit.
2. understand how to examine and amend an L/C.
3. master the writing skills of making amendment to the L/C or extension of the L/C and the relevant sentences and expressions.
4. be able to write reply letters to the above for both buyers and sellers.

Introduction

信用证是国际贸易中的一种约束受益人和银行行为的法律文件，是银行依照进口人的要求和指示或代表其自身，开给出口人（收益人）的在单证相符的条件下承诺支付或承兑汇票或发票金额的文件。信用证是国际贸易最常用的付款方式之一，在采用信用证付款时，一般要经过以下几个步骤：

1. 买卖双方签订销售合同，明确规定采用信用证结算方式。

2. 进口商向当地银行提出申请，在外汇管制国家，申请人还必须向外汇管理部提出用汇申请。在提出申请时，进口商还要缴纳若干押金或提供其他担保。

3. 开证行将信用证开给出口商所在地的分行或代理行，并请他们办理信用证通知事宜。

4. 通知行核对信用证上的印鉴或密押无误后，将信用证交给受益人。

5. 受益人将信用证与贸易合同核对无误后，立即备货装运，并取得运输单据，开出汇票，在信用证有效期内向当地银行交单议付。

6. 议付行将单据与信用证核对无误后，按汇票金额扣除利息和手续费后付款给受益人，并将从出口商手中取得的有关单据寄交给开证行索偿。

7. 开证行在审查单据无误后，偿付给议付行。

8. 开证行通知进口商赎单，进口商付款赎单后，凭提单向船公司提货，交易结束。

信用证有不同类型：

1. 根据开证行是否可以不经有关当事人同意撤销或修改信用证，可以分为可撤销信用证和不可撤销信用证。信用证没有注明可持续或不可撤销的，应视为不可撤销信用证。

2. 根据信用证是否有另一家银行加保兑分为保兑信用证和不可保兑信用证。

3. 根据信用证付款方式的不同分为即期付款信用证（L/C by sight payment）、延期付款信用证（L/C by deferred payment）、承兑信用证（L/C by acceptance）和议付信用证（L/C by negotiation）。

4. 根据信用证的全部或部分金额可否转让给第三者使用，分为可转让信用证（Transferable L/C）和不可转让信用证（Untransferable L/C）。

5. 其他形式信用证，如循环信用证（Revolving L/C）、红条款信用证（Red Clause L/C）、背对背信用证（Back to Back L/C）、对开信用证等（Reciprocal L/C）。

信用证审核是履行信用证付款合同的重要环节。审核信用证要依据合同，信用证依据买卖双方所订合同开立，所以其内容应与买卖合同内容相符。审核信用证要遵循UCP，外贸业务员审核信用证时，应遵循UCP600的规定来确定是否可以接受信用证条款。审核信用证还要全面考虑业务实践情况，这里的业务实际情况，是指信用证条款对安全收汇的影响程度、进口国的法令和法规以及申请人的商业习惯等。

审核信用证的基本要点如下：

1. 信用证本身的审核：

   1) 信用证的性质：是否为不可撤销。

   2) 适用惯例：是否申明所适用的国际惯例规则。

   3) 信用证的有效性：检查是否存在限制生效及其他保留条款，注意电开信用证是否为简电信用证。

   4) 信用证当事人：对开证申请人和受益人的名称和地址要仔细加以核对。

   5) 信用证到期日和到期地点：到期日应符合买卖合同的规定，一般为装运后15天或20天，到期地点一定要规定在出口商所在地以便做到及时交单。

2. 专项审核：

   1) 信用证金额、币种、付款期限规定是否与合同一致。

   2) 商品品名、货号、规格、数量规定是否与合同一致。

   3) 信用证中的装运条款包括装运期限、装运港、卸货港、分批装运之规定是否与合同一致。

   4) 对信用证项下要求受益人提交议付的单据通常包括：商业发票、保险单、海运提单、装箱单、原产地证明、检验证书以及其他证明文件，要注意单据由谁出具、能否出具，信用证对单据是否有特殊要求，单据的规定是否与合同条款一致，前后是否有矛盾。

CHAPTER VIII   ESTABLISHMENT OF L/C AND AMENDMENT TO L/C

Writing Strategy

要求改证的信函可以分为以下几个部分：
1. 确认收到信用证，同时指出其中有不符点。
2. 详述不符点的内容并提出如何修改。
3. 如果是我方的责任，道歉；如果不是，省略这一步骤。
4. 要求尽快修改，并期待尽早装船。

Lesson 19

(A) Urging Establishment of L/C (1)

合同一旦签署，如付款方式为信用证，应当催促买方及时开出信用证。为尽量避免因修改信用证产生费用和麻烦，买方通常会在请银行开立信用证之前，发一份开立信用证的申请书（L/C application）或草稿件（L/C draft），给供货方确认是否与合同一致。

From: Celia
To: Josef
Date: 2018-01-07
Subject: L/C for jogging order

Dear Josef,

Full amount L/C must be opened to Taizin latest at one month before delivery time (Dec. 25, 2017 latest).

The goods will be all ready and scheduled to take the vessel date of 21st Jan., 2018 and 28th Jan., 2018.

Pls arrange the L/C to us latest on Jan. 8, 2018 or the goods will not be shipped as scheduled.

Pls find attached Sales Contract and Proforma Invoice. The stipulations in the relevant credit should strictly conform to the terms in Sales Contract.

Thank you for your cooperation.

Best regards,
Celia
(CC: Mr. Benjamin Chan)

(B) Urging Establishment of L/C (2)

此封信续接此案例，由老板亲自解释原因，原因详细：办理海关手续及提前预订舱位。办理海关手续复杂，所以信用证应早开。

From: Benjamin
To: Josef
Date: 2018-01-08
Subject: L/C for jogging order

Dear Josef,

China Customs is very strict now. Shoe photos must be in our documents to Customs. They request Packing List & Invoice & L/C with official signature to avoid false tax refund. They also randomly come to inspect shipment. Also, each carton each PO must have tracking number for Customs to follow up. Normally L/C reaches us 30 days prior to shipment date. If you cannot open 30 days in advance, please open L/C at least 14 days before shipment. So we have enough time to do customs documentation & shipment booking ahead.

In addition to Celia's mail, there is still room available on July 2 vessel. Please work & PUSH your forwarder. Otherwise next vessel is on July 6.

Best regards,
Benjamin

CHAPTER VIII ESTABLISHMENT OF L/C AND AMENDMENT TO L/C

1. **urge** *vt.* 催促，劝说

   Recently they have been urging us for execution of their order for 3,000 gross pencils.
   最近他们一直在催促我们履行有关三千罗铅笔的订单。（1 罗 =12 打）
   Your are urged to give an early reply to our enquiry for groundnuts.
   请早日答复我们有关花生的询盘。

2. **establishment** *n.* 开立；建立

   We are arranging for the establishment of the relative L/C with the bank at this end.
   我们正安排此地银行开立有关信用证。
   We take this opportunity to approach you for the establishment of trade relations with you. 我们借此机会与你们联系，希望与你们建立贸易关系。

3. **jogging** *n.* 慢跑（此处指跑步运动鞋）

   I dislike jogging early in the morning. 我不喜欢早晨慢跑。

4. **full amount L/C** 全额信用证

   Payment is to be made against sight draft drawn under a confirmed, irrevocable, divisible and transferable L/C without recourse for the full amount.
   付款方式为保兑的、不可撤销的、可分割的、可转让的、无权追索的全部金额即期信用证支付。

5. **stipulation** *n.* 规定；约定；条款；契约

   The stipulations in the relative credit should strictly conform to the terms stated in our S/C. 信用证条款必须严格与合同条款一致。
   The transaction is concluded on the stipulation that L/C (should) be opened 30 days before the commencement of shipment.
   这笔交易必须包括一项条款，即信用证必须在装运开始前开立。
   stipulate *v.* 规定
   作不及物动词时与 for 连用。以 payment, shipment, quality 等名词或 that 引起的从句做宾语时，则不用 for，另外 that 从句用虚拟语气。
   We note that your order stipulates direct shipment. 我们知道你方规定直达轮装运。
   The contract stipulates that the goods (should) be shipped entire.
   合同规定货物全部装运。

6. **conform** *v.* 使一致；符合，遵照

   作及物动词时，宾语后接介词 to。

It is necessary to conform the specifications to the requirements. 规格与所需求的货一致是非常必要的。

The quality must conform to (with) the sample. 质量必须与样品一致。

conformity *n.* 符合，一致

主要用于 in conformity with 和 in conformity to 两个词组，二者均作"和……相一致；依照"解，前者较后者更普通。

This is not in conformity with our arrangement. 这与我们的安排不一致。

In conformity with (to) our desire to promote business, we have accepted your offer of 50 tons wool. 为了符合促进业务的愿望，我们已接受你方五十吨羊毛的报盘。

7. **false tax refund** 虚假退税

8. **tracking number /tacking No.** 查询号

便于查询的一个编号，在寄快件时，邮单上会有一个号码，可供查询邮单的递送状态；也可以是订单的内部编号。

We are pleased to send our samples to you including Art. HC13097，Art. HC808B301 by DHL on Nov. 17 and its tracking No. is QH12345.

兹通知贵方我方将复制的货号为 HC13097 和 HC808B301 的样品已由敦豪快递运出，查询号为 QH12345。

I. Translate the following expressions into Chinese or vice versa.

1. full amount L/C
2. establishment of L/C
3. as scheduled
4. false tax refund
5. open L/C
6. 条款
7. 包装单
8. 预先
9. 与……一致
10. 信用证申请书

II. Choose the best answer.

(   ) 1. We assure you that any further orders from you will _____ our prompt attention.

A. be taken   B. have   C. accept   D. be received

CHAPTER VIII ESTABLISHMENT OF L/C AND AMENDMENT TO L/C

(　　) 2. We have just received your email of Mar. 28 covering the _____ tin foil sheets（锡箔纸）.
    A. caption   B. captioning   C. captioned   D. captain

(　　) 3. We regret to inform you that we _____ your L/C covering the above sales confirmation till today.
    A. not receive   B. haven't received
    C. do not receive   D. received

(　　) 4. To avoid subsequent amendment, please see that the stipulations in the relative L/C _____ in strict conformity _____ the terms in our S/C.
    A. should be, to   B. be, with   C. are, with   D. is, to

(　　) 5. With regard _____ Contract No. 128, we are agreeable _____ D/P terms of payment.
    A. to, for   B. to, to   C. in, to   D. for, for

(　　) 6. We would call your attention _____ we have not received the amount of USD1,800 _____ the 20% of freight due.
    A. for that, for   B. to that, to
    C. for the fact that, to   D. to the fact that, for

(　　) 7. You _____ to send payment by 18 August at the latest.
    A. are requested   B. request
    C. are requesting   D. requesting us

(　　) 8. The clause is _____ approval by relevant authorities.
    A. subject to   B. subjected to
    C. subjects to   D. subjecting to

III. Translate the following sentences into English.
1. 请注意第 FA156 号销售合同项下的 20,000 个箱子备妥已久，但至今我们仍未收到你方有关信用证。
2. 若你方未在本月底前开来信用证，延期装运无法避免。
3. 你们所报货物的规格与我们询盘中的规格不符。
4. 目录和样品已由敦豪快递寄出，查询号为 QD1234。
5. 我们要求你方尽快开证，以便我方能装上 10 日左右到达此地的直达轮。

Lesson 20

Amend the L/C with Correct Amount

卖方收到信用证，首先要详细审证，看信用证条款是否与销售合同条款一致。如在信用证中发现差异或软条款，则应通知买方予以修改，不管有无异议，也要给买方信用证确认函（L/C open note）。卖方根据《跟单信用证统一惯例》逐项审核，包括对信用证本身的审核和专项审核，专项审核是指审核信用证的金额、币种、付款期限、商品名称、货号、规格、数量、装运条款和提交议付单证等是否与合同一致。

From: Winnie
To: Josef
Subject: amend the L/C with correct amount

Dear Josef/Vladimir,

Re: Revised S/C & PI for FW 2018 order

We regret to inform you that we just found out some payments (US$1547) were missed into our previous 07DE-790A S/C, PI and L/C open note.

1) Bulgaria: US$1,338.75 was missed
2) Hungary: US$208.25 was missed.

Now we have updated the S/C, PI & L/C open note, pls find & review the attached latest 18DE-S/C, PI and L/C open note.
Kindly note this S/C & PI # 18DE-790B replaces & supersedes the previous 18DE-790 & 18DE-790A, which is considered as null & void. Reason: correct the total amount.

Pls understand and amend the L/C with correct mount.

Sorry for the inconveniences caused to you, and thank you very much for your kind help.

Best regards,
Winnie
(CC: Mr. Benjamin Chan)

CHAPTER VIII ESTABLISHMENT OF L/C AND AMENDMENT TO L/C

1. **amend** *v.* 修改

   Please amend your L/C to allow partial shipments and transshipment.
   请修改信用证允许分批装运和转船。
   Please amend the amount of the L/C to read "5% more or less allowed".
   请将信用证中的金额改为"允许增减5%"。
   amendment *n.* 修改，修改书
   We have instructed our bank to make an amendment to the L/C No. 378 as requested.
   我方已通知银行按要求修改378号信用证。

2. **missed into** 使……误认为

   He missed me into thinking he was rich. 他使我误认为他很有钱。

3. **supersede** *vt.* 取代，代替；紧接着……而到来
            vi. 推迟行动

   We should supersede outdated regulations and customs. 我们必须废弃陈规旧习。
   Other documents may supersede this document. 其他单据可以代替这份单据。

4. **null & void** 无效

   A clause assigning the benefit of insurance of the goods in favor of the carrier or any similar clause shall be null and void.
   将货物的保险利益转让给承运人的条款或者类似条款均无效。

I. Translate the following expressions into Chinese or vice versa.

   1. L/C open note
   2. revised S/C
   3. supersede
   4. correct the total amount
   5. cause inconvenience
   6. 使……误认为
   7. 信用证的随后修改
   8. 信用证条款
   9. 查询号
   10. 无效

II. Fill in the blanks with proper prepositions.

   1. We note with regret that your L/C 125 was opened _____ US$50,000 only.

Please have it amended _____ our S/C SF52, adding "5% tolerance allowed" _____ the items of quantity and amount.

2. All the banking charges outside China should be _____ the buyer's account.

3. _____ our disappointment, we haven't received your L/C _____ your order No. 123.

4. In view _____ our long-term business relations, we are prepared to wait _____ your L/C, which must reach us prior _____ November 23.

5. We apologize _____ you _____ the trouble we have caused you.

6. Any loss arising _____ the delay _____ shipment will be _____ your account.

7. To avoid subsequent amendments, please make sure that the L/C stipulations strictly conform _____ the terms of our contract.

8. We have instructed our bank to make an amendment _____ the L/C No. 378 as requested.

III. Translate the following sentences into English.

1. 我们发现你方 99 号信用证金额短缺 500 英镑，请按合同金额予以修改。
2. 我们要求你方在数量前加上"大约"字样。
3. "运费预付"应改为"运费到付"。
4. 关于 6523 号信用证，请通知银行将佣金改为 5%，不胜感激。
5. 请按下述意见修改 310 号信用证：金额增至 24,000 美元，删去"不许转船"字样。

Lesson 21

(A) Amendment to L/C

信用证在交单的时候，经常会有不符点产生。在这种情况下，如果不是特别严重的问题，只要得到客户的确认，银行是可以继续偿付的。但是开立信用证一般在生产前，订单操作过程中会出现各种变数，需要请买方合作，修改或延期信用证。

CHAPTER VIII ESTABLISHMENT OF L/C AND AMENDMENT TO L/C

From: Winnie
To: Josef
RE: L/C for FW2018 order

Dear Josef,

After contacting bank, we are informed that there are some discrepancies in the L/C. Kindly make the following necessary amendments as early as possible so as to facilitate our shipping arrangement.

1) 45A GOODS

CONSIGNEE D: 1795 PAIRS USD11,071.25 (IN THE L/C)—WRONG

CONSIGINEE D: 1795 PAIRS USD12,410.00—CORRECT (PLS AMEND THE L/C as it is)

CONSIGNEE H: 750 PAIRS: USD4,875.25 (IN THE L/C)—WRONG

CONSIGNEE H: 750 PAIRS: USD5,083.50—CORRECT (PLS AMEND THE L/C as it is)

The L/C has 5% tolerance, but it is only workable for one shipment only, and unworkable for FW2018 order, as it has 9 shipments totally, the 5% tolerance should be used separately for each shipment. For example, if 5% tolerance is used for 11,071.25, then the amount is 11,624.81, which is less than 12,410.00. Pls amend the L/C as the above. Thanks.

2) 47A

I) ALBERTSLUND, DENMARK (IN THE L/C)—WRONG

But as per Eva's email dated on 7/23, the port of entry should be "GLOSTRUP" instead of ALBERTSLUND. The port of entry on the B/L will be different from L/C stated, and it will cause the discrepancy. Pls amend the L/C.

3) 44C LATEST DATE OF SHIPMENT: 19 AUG. 10

We are rushing the goods for FW2018 currently; the goods of Croatia & Denmark are under making and will catch the vessel on time as per our L/C.

But we have the big difficulty on the other shipment, as there are some issues with the same outsoles of 116DD, 207DD & 407DD, and need remake, the new outsoles will be ready around on Aug. 15. And we will try our best to rush these goods on Aug. 18 to meet the fastest vessel on 8/22.

Please kindly extend the shipment from 8/19 to 8/25. (We will deliver the goods to Xiamen port on 8/19 to catch the 8/22 shipment, but please get the 8/25 for us, as sometimes the vessel may be delayed by something uncontrolled, such as the bad weather.)

Kindly review & comment ASAP.

Best regards,
Winnie
(CC: Mr. Benjamin Chan)

(B) Amending L/C to Allow Transshipment

From: Benjamin
To: Josef
Subject: allow transshipment

Dear Josef,

Sorry for the late email.

1) We have contacted the forwarder. We would deliver the goods to forwarder before Aug. 19, but we were informed that the vessel is not available on Aug. 19.

The fastest vessel they can arrange for us is Aug. 22, but the arrival date is same. Pls understand and amend the L/C. Thanks.

2) Transshipment:
Noted you will change the transshipment back to ALLOWED.

Pls rush to amend the L/C based on the above instruction. Thanks.

Best regards,
Benjamin

CHAPTER VIII ESTABLISHMENT OF L/C AND AMENDMENT TO L/C

Notes

1. **discrepancy** *n.* 不符；矛盾；不符点

    Please amend the discrepancies in the above L/C. 请修改上述信用证中的不符点。

    In case of any discrepancy between unit prices and amounts, unit prices shall govern.

    如果单价与总金额之间有出入，应以单价为准。

2. **facilitate** *v.* 使容易，便于

    Please open your L/C immediately to facilitate our shipping arrangement.

    请立即开立信用证以便我们安排装船。

    注意：facilitate 是使动作容易，而不是使人容易动作。

    误：This will facilitate you to apply for the import license.

    正：This will facilitate your applying for the import license.

3. **consignee** *n.* 收货人

    I used to dispatch telex to shipper and the consignee to inform them change of our schedule and other information.

    我过去经常向寄货人和取货人发出电传，通知他们船期的更改及其他消息。

4. **5% tolerance** 5% 左右的公差，即（信用证额度、产品数量或单价等）所允许的浮动幅度。

5. **Albertslund** 阿尔贝特斯兰，是丹麦的一个自治市，位于西兰岛东部、哥本哈根以西。

    Glostrup 格洛斯楚普，是丹麦的一个自治市，位于西兰岛东北部、哥本哈根以西。

6. **extend** *vt.* 延长，使展期；扩展；给予

    extend...to... 将……延长到……（日期）

    The L/C expires of November 30th, and we hope you will extend the validity date to December 15th.

    该信用证于 11 月 30 日期满，我们希望你将其有效期延至 12 月 15 日。

    extension *n.* 延长，展期

    Extension commission will be for your account. 展延手续费将由你方负担。

    We have contacted our customer today asking for a two-week extension of the L/C covering Order No. 8982.

    我们已与客户联系，要求他们将 8982 号订单信用证的有效期延长两周。

    extension advice 延期通知

    extension of an L/C 信用证的展期

信用证中都规定有装运日期和到期日期，有时卖方未能及时将货物备妥待运，或买方由于某种原因要求延迟装运，这时卖方将不得不要求买方将信用证中的装运日期和到期日期分别延长，即信用证的展期或信用证的展延。

7. transshipment *n.* 转运

Transshipment will be made at Hong Kong. 转船将在香港进行。

transship *v.* 转运

The goods should be transshipped at Kaohsiung. 货物将在高雄转船。

I. Translate the following expressions into Chinese or vice versa.

1. discrepancy in weight
2. extension advice
3. extension of an L/C
4. make transshipment
5. instead of
6. 收货人
7. 到期
8. 溢短差额
9. 按约定
10. 修改通知书

II. Choose the best answer.

(　　) 1. An L/C requests all the following documents except _____.
  A. commercial invoice   B. bills of lading
  C. sales letter   D. packing list

(　　) 2. The term CIF should be followed by _____.
  A. port of origin   B. port of shipment
  C. port of destination   D. port of loading

(　　) 3. The bank who opens the L/C required by the buyer is called _____.
  A. paying bank   B. issuing bank
  C. negotiating bank   D. notifying bank

(　　) 4. _____ the goods have been ready for shipment for some time, please establish the relative L/C _____ our favor as soon as possible.
  A. Because, on   B. Because, in   C. As, in   D. As, on

(　　) 5. Failure to establish the L/C _____ will _____ the fulfillment of this order.

CHAPTER VIII   ESTABLISHMENT OF L/C AND AMENDMENT TO L/C

    A. on time, effect   B. on time, affect on
    C. in time, affect   D. in time, effect on

( ) 6. As the shipment date _____, we must point out that unless your L/C reaches us by the end of this month, we shall not be able to effect shipment within the _____ time.
    A. is approaching, contracting B. is approaching, contracted
    C. approached, contracting   D. approached, contracted

( ) 7. Your L/C calls for an insurance amount for 120% of the invoice value. _____ we would request you to amend the insurance clause.
    A. The case is like this   B. The case being it
    C. Such being the case   D. Such is the case

( ) 8. Due to unforeseen difficulties, we find it impossible to make shipment in July, and would appreciate _____ the shipment date and validity of your L/C to May 31 and June 15 _____.
    A. you to extend, respectively B. you to extend, respective
    C. your extending, respectively D. your extending, respective

( ) 9. As arranged, we would ask you to open an confirmed and irrevocable letter of credit in _____ favor and shall hand over shipping documents _____ acceptance of our draft.
    A. our, against   B. our, for
    C. your, against   D. your, for

( ) 10. You must be aware that the terms and conditions of a contract once _____ should be strictly _____, failure to abide by them will mean violation of contract.
    A. signed, observed   B. signed, observing
    C. signing, observed   D. signing, observing

( ) 11. The extension of the time of shipment will facilitate our _____ the goods.
    A. preparing B. preparedness C. readiness D. ready

( ) 12. The goods should be transshipped _____ Kaohsiung.
    A. via   B. in   C. through   D. at

III. Translate the following sentences into English.

  1. 我们遗憾地发现有些条款与合同中的条款不符。
  2. 受益人应为"太平洋贸易公司"，而不是"东方贸易有限公司"。
  3. 买方没有延展信用证，而是要求我们立刻装运。

4. 请将信用证上的金额修改为"允许 5% 的上下幅度"。
5. 请把该证装运期展延至 2021 年 12 月 15 日，议付期展延至 12 月 31 日。
6. 你方 4435 号信用证已到，但经审核后发现不准转船和分批装运，请立即修改你们的信用证。

Business Link

MT700 信用证中的基本项目

M/O	Tag	Field Name（项目名称）	Meaning in Chinese（中文含义）
M	27	SEQUENCE OF TOTAL	报文页次
M	40A	FORM OF DOCUMENTARY CREDIT	跟单信用证形式
M	20	DOCUMENTARY CREDIT NUMBER	信用证号码
O	23	REFERENCE TO PRE-ADVICE	预先通知号码
O	31C	DATE OF ISSUE	开证日期
M	31D	DATE AND PLACE OF EXPIRY	有效期和有效地点
O	51A	APPLICANT BANK	开证银行
M	50	APPLICANT	开证申请人
M	59	BENEFICIARY	受益人
M	32B	CURRENCY CODE, AMOUNT	信用证结算的货币和金额
O	39A	PERCENTAGE CREDIT AMOUNT TOLERANCE	信用证金额上下浮动允许的最大范围
O	39B	MAXIMUM CREDIT AMOUNT	信用证最大限制金额
O	39C	ADDITIONAL MOUNTS COVERED	额外金额
M	41a	AVAILABLE WITH…BY…	指定的有关银行及信用证兑付的方式
O	42C	DRAFTS AT…	汇票付款日期
O	42a	DRAWEE	汇票付款人
O	42M	MIXED PAYMENT DETAILS	混合付款条款

CHAPTER VIII ESTABLISHMENT OF L/C AND AMENDMENT TO L/C

(Continued)

M/O	Tag	Field Name（项目名称）	Meaning in Chinese（中文含义）
O	42P	DEFERRED PAYMENT DETAILS	延期付款条款
O	43P	PARTIAL SHIPMENTS	分装条款
O	43T	TRANSSHIPMENT	转运条款
O	44A	LOADING ON BOARD/DISPATCH/TAKING IN CHARGE AT/FROM	装船、发运和接受监管的地点
O	44B	FOR TRANSPORTATION TO...	货物发运的最终地
O	44C	LATEST DATE OF SHIPMENT	最后装船期
O	44D	SHIPMENT PERIOD	船期
O	45A	DESCRIPTION OF GOODS AND/OR SERVICES	货物描述
O	46A	DOCUMENTS REQUIRED	单据要求
O	47A	ADDITIONAL CONDITIONS	特别条款
O	71B	CHARGES	费用情况
O	48	PERIOD FOR PRESENTATION	交单期限
M	49	CONFIRMATION INSTRUCTIONS	保兑指示
O	53a	REIMBURSEMENT BANK	偿付行
O	78	INSTRUCTION TO THE PAYING / ACCEPTING/NEGOTIATING BANK	给付款行、承兑行、议付行的指示
O	57a	"ADVISE THROUGH" BANK	通知行
O	72	SENDER TO RECEIVER INFORMATION	附言

Skill Training

Exercise I. Write a letter in English asking for amendments to the following letter of credit by checking it against the terms of the given contract.

售 货 合 同

SALES CONTRACT

合同号码：

卖　方：AAA IMPORT AND EXPORT CO.　　买　方：BBB TRADING CO.

| 222 JIANGUO ROAD | P.O. BOX 203 |
| DALIAN, CHINA | GDANSK, POLAND |

兹经买卖双方同意由卖方出售买方购进之下列货物，并按下列条款签订本合同：

（This Sales Contract is made out as per the following terms and conditions confirmed by both parties.）

商品名称与规格 Commodity & Specifications	数量 Quantity	单价 Unit Price	金额 Amount
65% POLYESTER 35% COTTON LADIES SKIRTS		CIF GDANSK	
STYLE NO. A101	200 DOZ	USD60/DOZ	USD12,000.00
STYLE NO. A102	400 DOZ	USD84/DOZ	USD33,600.00
ORDER NO. HMW0501			
Total Value: USD FORTY FIVE THOUSAND AND SIX HUNDRED ONLY			

Time of shipment: DECEMBER, 2014

Transhipment: ALLOWED

Partial shipments: ALLOWED

Port of loading: DALIAN

Port of destination: GDANSK

Payment: BY TRANSFERABLE L/C PAYABLE 60 DAYS AFTER B/L DATE, REACHING THE SELLERS 45 DAYS BEFORE THE SHIPMENT.

Insurance: TO BE EFFECTED BY THE BUYER FOR 110% INVOICE VALUE COVERING F.P.A. RISKS OF PICC CLAUSE.

Force majeure: the Seller shall not be held liable for failure or delay in delivery of the entire lot or a portion of the Commodity under this contract in consequence of any force majeure incidents.

Other conditions: 略

David King   苏进

Buyers (Signature)   Sellers (Signature)

CHAPTER VIII ESTABLISHMENT OF L/C AND AMENDMENT TO L/C

LETTER OF CREDIT

40A FORM OF DC:	IRREVOCABLE
20 DC NO:	70/1/5822
31C DATE OF ISSUE:	141007
40E APPLICABLE RULES	UCP LATEST VERSION
31D EXPIRY DATE AND PLACE:	150115, POLAND
50 APPLICANT:	BBB TRADING CO.
	P.O. BOX 203
	GDANSK, POLAND
59 BENEFICIARY:	AAA IMPORT AND EXPORT CO.
	222 JIANGUO ROAD,
	DALIAN, CHINA
32B DC AMT:	CURRENCY USD AMOUNT 45,600.00
41D AVAILABLE WITH/BY:	BANK OF CHINA DALIAN BRANCH BY DEF PAYMENT
42P DEFERRED PAYM. DET.	60 DAYS AFTER B/L DATE
43P PARTIAL SHIPMENTS:	NOT ALLOWED
43T TRANSSHIPMENT:	ALLOWED
44A LOADING IN CHARGE:	SHANGHAI
44B FOR TRANSPORT TO:	GDANSK
44C LATEST DATE OF SHIPMENT:	141231

45A DESCRIPT. OF GOODS:

   65% POLYESTER 35% COTTON LADIES SHIRTS

   STYLE NO. A101 200 DOZ @USD60/DOZ

   STYLE NO. A102 400 DOZ @USD84/DOZ

   ALL OTHER DETAILS OF GOODS ARE AS PER CONTRACT NO. LT07060 DATED AUG. 10, 2014.

   DELIVERY TERMS: CIF GDANSK (INCOTERMS 2000)

46A/DOCUMENTS REQUIRED:

   1. COMMERICAL INVOICE MANUALLY SIGNED IN 2 ORIGINALS PLUS 1 COPY MADE OUT TO DDD TRADING CO., P.O. BOX 211, GDANSK, POLAND

   2. FULL SET (3/3) OF ORIGINAL CLEAN ON BOARD BILL OF LADING PLUS 3/3 NONNEGOTIABLE COPIES, MADE OUT TO THE ORDER OF ISSUING BANK AND BLANK ENDORSED, NOTIFY THE APPLICANT, MARKED FREIGHT

PREPAID MENTIONING GROSS WEIGHT AND NET WEIGHT.

 3. ASSORTMENT LIST IN 2 ORIGINALS PLUS 1 COPY.

 4. CERTIFICATE OF ORIGIN IN 1 ORIGINAL PLUS 2 COPIES SIGNED BY CCPIT.

 5. MARINE INSURANCE POLICY IN THE CURRENCY OF THE CREDIT ENDORSED IN BLANK FOR CIF VALUE PLUS 30 PCT MARGIN COVERING ALL RISKS OF PICC CLAUSES INDICATING CLAIMS PAYABLE IN POLAND.

47A ADDITIONAL CONDITINONS:

 +ALL DOCUMENTS MUST BE ISSUED IN ENGLISH.

 +SHIPMENTS MUST BE EFFECTED BY FCL.

 +B/L MUST SHOWING SHIPPING MARKS: BBB, S/C LT07060，GDAND, C/NO.

 +ALL DOCS MUST NOT SHOW THIS L/C NO. 70/1/5822.

 +FOR DOCS WHICH DO NOT COMPLY WITH L/C TERMS AND CONDITIONS, WE SHALL DEDUCT FROM THE PROCEEDS A CHARGE OF EUR50.00 PAYABLE IN USD EQUIVALENT PLUS ANY INCCURED SWIFT CHARGES IN CONNECTION WITH.

71B DETAILS OF CHARGES:	ALL BANKING COMM/CHARGES OUTSIDE POLAND ARE ON BENEFICIARY ACCOUNT.
48 PERIOD FOR PRESENTATION:	15 DAYS AFTER B/L DATE, BUT WITHIN L/C VALIDITY.
49 CONFIRMATION:	WITHOUT
78 INSTRUCTIONS:	WE SHALL REIMBURSE AS PER YOUR INSTRUCTIONS.
72 SEND TO REC. INFO:	CREDIT SUBJECT TO ICC PUBL. 600

Exercise II. Write a letter in English asking for amendments to the following letter of credit by checking it against the terms of the given contract.

HONG KONG & SHANGHAI BANKING CORPORATION
QUEEN'S ROAD CENTRAL, P.O. BOX 64, HK
TEL: 852-23034578 FAX: 851-23039742

Advised through: Bank of China
      Shanghai Branch
To: SHANGHAI TEXTILES IMP. & EXP. CORPORATION

CHAPTER VIII   ESTABLISHMENT OF L/C AND AMENDMENT TO L/C

27 ZHONGSHAN ROAD, SHANGHAI, CHINA

Applicant: SUPERB AIM (HONG KONG) LTD.

RM. 450 FUNGLEE COMMBLDG. KOWLOON, HONG KONG

Dear Sirs,

We hereby open our irrevocable L/C No. CN3099/714 in your favor for a sum not exceeding about HKD540,000.00 (SAY HK DOLLARS FIVE HUNDRED FORTY THOUSAND ONLY) available by your draft drawn on HSBC at 30 days after sight accompanied by the following documents:

1. Signed Commercial Invoice in triplicate.
2. Packing list in quadruplicate.
3. 2/3 clean on board B/L made out to order notify the above mentioned applicant and marked "Freight Collect" dated not later than October 31, 2006. From Shanghai to Hong Kong, partial shipment are not permitted.
4. Insurance policy in 2 copies covering All Risks and War Risks for 150% invoice value as per the relevant ocean marine cargo clauses of the PICC dated 1981/01/01.
5. Certificate of Origin issued by China Council for the Promotion of International Trade.
6. A certificate issued by the beneficiary and countersigned by buyer's representative Mr. Jeremiah, his signature must be verified by opening bank, certifying the quality to conform to sample submitted on 7th June, 2014.

DESCRIPTION OF GOODS:

Textile, twill 2/1 108 × 54/20 × 20 59", Total 10,000 meters. Packed in cartons of ten meters, USD54.00 per meter CIFC2HK.

SPECIAL INSTRUCTIONS:

1) Shipping advice to be sent by fax to the applicant immediately after the shipment stating our L/C No., shipping marks, name of vessel, goods description and amount as well as the bill of lading No. and date. A copy of such advice must accompany the original documents presented for negotiation.

2) 1/3 clean on board B/L sent to applicant by DHL within 24 hours after shipment.

3) We undertake to honour all the drafts drawn in compliance with the terms of this credit if such drafts to be presented at our counter on or before Oct. 31st, 2014.

4) The negotiating bank is kindly requested to forward all documents to us (HONG KONG & SHANGHAI BANKING CORPORATION QUEEN'S ROAD CENTRAL, P.O. BOX 64, HK) in one lot by airmail.

It is subject to the Uniform Customs and Practice for Documentary Credit (1993)

Revision, International Chamber of Commerce Publication No. 600.

Yours faithfully,

For HONG KONG & SHANGHAI BANKING CORPORATION

SHANGHAI TEXTILES IMP. & EXP. CORP.
27 ZHONGSHAN ROAD, SHANGHAI, CHINA
TEL : 86-21-63218467   FAX : 86-21-63291267

SALES CONFIRMATION

No. : ST 060311
Date: Aug. 15, 2014

TO: SUPERBAIM (HONG KONG) LTD.
RM. 504 FUNGLEE COMM BLDG KOWLOON, HONG KONG

We hereby confirm having sold to you the following goods on terms and conditions as stated below.

NAME OF COMMODITY: textile
SPECIFICATION: Twill 2/1 108 × 54/20 × 20 59"
PACKING: Packed in cartons of ten meters
QUANTITY: Total 10,000 meters
UNIT PRICE: USD54.00 per meter CIFC2 HK
TOTAL AMOUNT: USD540,000.00
SHIPMENT: During Oct./Nov. 2014 from Shanghai to HK with partial shipments permitted.
INSURANCE: To be covered by the seller for 110% of total value against all risks and war risk as per the relevant ocean marine cargo clauses of the PICC dated 1981/01/01.
PAYMENT: The buyer should open through a bank acceptable to the seller an irrevocable L/C payable at 30 days after B/L date to reach the seller 30 days before the month of shipment valid for negotiation in China until the 15th day after the date of shipment.
REMARKS: Please sign and return one copy for our file.

CHAPTER VIII ESTABLISHMENT OF L/C AND AMENDMENT TO L/C

The Buyer:
  Alice

The Seller:
  SHANGHAI TEXTILES IMP. & EXP. CORP.

Useful Expressions

可套用的句型：

1. 感谢来证

   Thank you for your L/C No. ××××× issued by ××××× dated ×××××.

   We are pleased to receive L/C No. ××××× established by ××××× dated ××××× against S/C No. ×××××.

   Thank you for your L/C No. ××××× issued/dated on ××××× covering the goods/shipment under contract No. ×××××.

   We have duly received your L/C No. 97531 but regretfully find it contains quite a few discrepancies. You are requested, therefore, to make the following amendments:

   We have received your L/C No. A-2234 but regret to say that we have found some discrepancies in the above mentioned L/C.

2. 列明不符点

   However, we are sorry to find it contains the following discrepancies.

   But the following points are in discrepancy with the stipulations of our S/C No. ×××××.

   Please add the word...before...

   Please delete the clause...and insert the wording...

   Pleased amend the...to...

   The amount should be...not / instead of...

   Please extend the shipment date and the validity of the L/C to...and...respectively.

3. 催促改证

   Thank you for your kind cooperation. Please see to it that the L/C amendment reach us before ××××× (date), failing which we shall not be able to effect punctual shipment.

   As the date of shipment is drawing near, please let us have your telex amendments without delay.

   As the stipulated time of shipments is drawing near, please make the requested amendments to the L/C as soon as possible so that we can effect shipment in time.

CHAPTER IX
PACKING & MARKING

Objectives:

After learning this chapter, you will

1. understand the importance of proper packing and terms of packing in foreign sales contract.
2. grasp the essential components of a letter on packing.
3. master typical sentences and expressions in writing letters on packing.

Introduction

　　商品包装是商品在生产和流通过程中保护商品品质完好和数量完整的一种手段。在对外贸易中，做好商品的包装和装潢，还能起到美化商品，提高出口商品的竞争能力，扩大销售的作用。进出口商品除散装货和裸装货外，大多数商品都需要包装，它不仅有助于销售，而且便于运输、储存和装卸，节约运费，减少破损。包装有两种形式：1. 外包装，即用于运输的包装；2. 内包装，即中小型的包装、盒子或销售包装。包装容器有：袋（bag）、麻袋（sack）、纸箱（carton）、箱子（case）、盒（box）、板条箱（crate）、桶（drum）、包（bale）、罐头（can 或 tin）、大玻璃瓶（carboy）、捆（bundle）、集装箱（container）、货盘（pallet）等。不同容器供不同商品使用，具有不同用途。

　　为了防止货物在运输途中的震动、破碎、受潮、锈损等，在包装中通常还使用纸屑、纸条、泡沫塑料等衬垫物。

　　在外包装上一般都印有运输标志，习称唛头。其目的是便于识别货物，以利于运输装卸和储存。运输标志一般包括三个部分。

　　1. 收货人的标志，包括目的港。如：

B　　C
LONDON
Nos.1-400

2. 当局所需要的官方标志。有些国家需要在每件货物的箱（包）上标有货物的生产国名，以及每箱的重量和尺寸。如：

  KUWAIT   G.W. 46KGS
  Nos.1-400   MEAS 100CM × 45CM × 45CM
  MADE IN CHINA   N.W. 43.5KGS

3. 特别指示或警告。为了货主和运输公司双方的利益，在包装上须印刷搬运方式、装货方式、起吊方式等特别指示或警告。

Writing Strategy

包装信函的写作步骤：
1. 提及货物及货物性质。
2. 对货物内、外包装的要求（说明包装方式、包装材料等）。
3. 感谢合作。

回复包装信函的写作步骤：
1. 感谢对方来函并告知对方回信的目的。
2. 提出有关包装的参考意见和解决办法。
3. 表示希望对方能够确认此包装意见和办法。

Lesson 22

Inner Packing & Labeling

  内包装，即中小型的包装、盒子或销售包装。实际业务中，产品的包装需严格按照购货合同的规定来进行。出口商品的包装要求各不相同，供货方应征得购货方同意的包装方式，或根据购货方的具体要求进行包装。

From: Jeremy Weiner @hotmail.com
To: alicia0618@tchina.com
Subject: inner packing requirements

Dear Alicia,

Thanks for your email. In order to avoid possible future trouble, we would like to make clear beforehand our packing requirements, especially inner packing as follows:

For ART. NO. HC13097, each pair must be on a strong good quality hanger and packed in a polybag then 24 pairs to a carton. The polybag can be self sourced and should be self sealing with a gummed strip. No health warning is required on this bag. Each foot must contain a woven insole label and a price label. Exact color instructions can be found in the instruction manual sent by separate mail. Attached with a Nylon string to each pair must be a hand tag with PRICE on the front and the bar code on the back. The BLACK hanger must have a multi coloured size sticker attached on the oval shape. Photos as below:

For ART. NO. HC808B301, each pair still need to be wrapped with tissue paper and packed in PLAIN WHITE SHOE BOX with finger hole. The shoes/tissue paper/shoe box should be with no reference of ×××××. After assessing this style, we have decided that the shoes are not required to be lined with cardboard skillets or tissue paper. This shoe should hold its own shape during transit without any additional packaging. Be sure to put the wording on the shoe box bottom both in English and in Italian.

Looking forward to your early reply.

Best regards,
Jeremy Weiner

CHAPTER IX PACKING & MARKING

1. **packing** *n.* 包装

   Your price is to include packing in crate, and delivery to our warehouse.
   贵方报价应包括板条箱包装费和到我方仓库的运费。

   pack *v.* 包装，把……装箱

   The pens are packed in boxes of one dozen each, 200 boxes to a wooden case.
   钢笔应装在盒子里，每盒装一打，每 200 盒装一木箱。

   与包装有关的用法如下：

   1) in... 用某种容器包装

      The goods must be packed in 5-ply strong paper bags as contracted.
      货物应按合同规定用五层坚固纸袋包装。

   2) in...of...each... 用某种容器包装，每件若干重量

      Men's Shirts are packed in wooden cases of 10 dozen each.
      男式衬衫用木箱装，每箱十打。

   3) in...each containing... 用某种容器包装，每件内装若干

      Nylon Socks are packed in wooden cases, each containing 50 dozen.
      尼龙袜用木箱包装，每箱装五十打。

   4) ...to... 某种商品装于某一容器中

      Folding Chairs are packed 2 pieces to a carton. 折叠椅两把装一个纸板箱。

   5) each...in...and...to... 每单位装某种容器，若干单位装另一种较大的容器

      Each pair of Nylon Socks is packed in a polybag and 12 pairs to a box.
      每双尼龙袜装一个塑料袋，十二双装一盒。

   6) ...to...and...to... 若干单位装某种较小的容器，若干单位装另一种较大的容器

      Pens are packed 12 pieces to a box and 200 boxes to a wooden case.
      钢笔十二支装一盒，二百盒装一木箱。

2. **polybag** 塑料袋

   Each pair of nylon socks is packed in a polybag and 12 pairs to a box.
   尼龙袜子每双包装用塑料袋包装，每 12 双装一个盒。

3. **woven insole label** 布标

4. **price label** 定价标签

5. **instruction manual** 使用手册，说明书

   Refer to the instruction manual before installation and operation.

请在安装和操作前阅读说明书。

6. **hang tag** 挂牌，吊牌

   指挂在产品上用以说明所用材料、规格、产品的牌子或公司联系方式等信息的纸质或 PVC 的标牌。

纸质挂牌

PVC 挂牌

7. **the BLACK hanger** 黑色挂钩

   一些鞋子需要用挂钩托住保持形状。

8. **wrapped with/in** 用……包装，包在……里

   For the above order, the goods should be packed in tin-lined water-proof woolen bale, each bale wrapped in oilcloth, and 10 bales packed in one case.

   这批货物必须装在内衬锡纸的防水毛纺布里，外用油毡布包，每十包装一箱。

9. **finger hole/grip hole** 指孔

10. **be lined with** 内衬

    Each carton is lined with a polythene sheet and secured by overall strapping.

    纸板箱均内衬一层聚乙烯塑料布，并用带子全面捆扎加固。

    lining *n.* 衬里，衬套，内层

    The wool sweaters must be packed each in a polythene bag with an inner lining of stout waterproof materials and then in cardboard box, 10 dozen to a carton.

    羊毛衫必须一件装一个聚乙烯塑料袋，内衬坚固防水材料，然后装入硬纸盒，10 打装一纸箱。

11. **hold shape** 保持形状

12. **additional packaging** 额外的包装费用

CHAPTER IX   PACKING & MARKING

I. Translate the following expressions into Chinese or vice versa.

1. hang tag
2. bar code
3. European size
4. price label
5. inner packing
6. 包装条款
7. 使用手册
8. 内衬……
9. 挂牌
10. 包装要求

II. Fill in the blanks in the following letter with the proper words given below.

| packed   warning   requirements   stand   secured   suitable   hang tag |

Dear Sirs,

As to our PO No. CE578 for 5,000 cartons of wool sweaters to be shipped to us during May, we would like to make clear our packing _____ as follows:

The packing should be novel, _____ for supermarket sales and each one should have _____, bar codes. One dozen should be _____ to a box with a cardboard tray inside, 20 boxes to a carton. The cartons should be strong enough to _____ the dropping test without breakage and _____ outside with plastic straps. On the left side of the carton there should be a _____ mark: "Do not use a hook."

We will email you the pictures of the bar codes and hang tags for each item next time. We trust that you can meet the above requirements and thank you in advance for your cooperation.

We look forward to your early reply.

Yours faithfully,
×××

III. Put the following into English.

1. 条形码贴于挂卡上以及贴于胶袋右上角。

2. 我们要求将每件女式衬衫装一个塑料袋，每 12 打装一有防水衬里的纸箱。
3. 我方能满足你方对包装的特殊要求，但额外包装费用须由你方负责。
4. 根据你方的建议，我们已改进了内包装，以满足你方市场消费者的需要。
5. 木箱上不需要印刷警告语。

Lesson 23

Outer Packing

外包装，即用于运输的包装。在外包装上一般都印有运输标志，习称唛头。唛头又分为主唛（或正唛 main marks）和侧唛（side marks）。正唛一般是由客户提供，通常由型号、图形（字母、数字及简单的文字）或收货单位简称、目的港、件数或批号等组成。而侧唛则显示商品的尺寸、毛重、净重等资料，用于客户在目的国收货拆柜后辨认货物之用。

From: Jeremy Weiner @hotmail.com
To: alicia0618@tchina.com
Sent: November 23, 2010
Subject: outer carton information

Dear Alicia,

  Thank you for your email of November 12 inquiring for outer packing.

  As regards outer carton, egg-crating within a carton is no longer permitted because we'll select goods through the punch panel on the side mark. This is to be replaced with 'S' crating. Please use a piece of 5-ply corrugated cardboard and curve the cardboard around the bulk goods to protect goods and strengthen the carton. Please see example below.

  Cartons should NOT be made from recyclable cardboard as such kinds of recycled materials are not strong enough to protect the goods from suffering the damp or damage during container transit/sea freight. We have already confirmed that the number of pairs per carton is 24—this cannot be changed.

CHAPTER IX   PACKING & MARKING

Cartons must be sealed with tape. Under no circumstances should staples be tied, stapled, glued or shrink wrapped. It does not need to be secured outside with plastic straps. All cartons must be perforated with a "punch panel" for ease of warehouse picking with a thumb tab for ease of opening. You will find the other detailed requirements for the carton in our attachment.

Please see separate instructions for shipping mark (main mark) and side marks in the attachment. We trust that you can meet the above requirements and thank you in advance for your cooperation.

Best regards,
Jeremy Weiner

PACKING INSTRUCTION FOR A.B.S.T

      Main mark   Side mark

With reference to the main and side mark of the above order, we would like to draw your special attention to the packing instructions listed as follows:

1. The carton label must be attached to the perforated end of the carton in the upper half of the perforation. Please see example below.

2. The carton perforations for the "punch panel" should only be 4-ply deep, leaving the 5th ply unperforated to assist with carton strength. The carton perforations should be no less than 7.5mm apart.

3. Silica gel packs—Our customers have requested that we can not use packets containing beads of silica gel as these can split open on the shop floor & can be dangerous. They have requested us to use Microban/Microgarde instead. Please affix one sticker per carton.

4. The pre-pack part of this order will require a red NEW PRODUCT label to be attached to the outer carton.

5. Please mark our initials in a diamond, under which the port of destination and our order number should be stenciled or printed.

1. **egg crate, egg-crate packing** 蛋格包装，像蛋一样一双双插入，如下图：

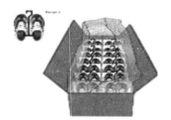

2. **punch panel** 冲孔

   是指在钢板、革、布、木板等材料上打出各种图形以适应不同的需求，具体有：十字孔、菱形孔、鱼鳞孔、八字孔、六方孔、冲孔板、长孔、四方孔、圆孔、冲孔板网、三角孔等。

3. **'S' crating** S 形纸板

4. **5-ply corrugated cardboard** 5 层瓦楞纸

5. **recyclable cardboard** 可回收纸板，再生纸板

   recycled materials 再生的材料

   As with our other boxed products, our cardboard boxes are both recycled and recyclable.

CHAPTER IX   PACKING & MARKING

如同我们的其他盒装产品一样,我们的纸箱都是可回收和循环再造的。

6. **be sealed with** 用……密封

   The powder must be packed in plastic bags and then put into drums which are to be sealed with adhesive tape.

   所有的粉末都要用塑料袋包装,并装到罐子里,罐子要用胶带封紧。

7. **to be secured with** 用……加固

   We do not object to packing in cartons, provided the flaps are glued down and the cartons secured with metal bands.

   如果箱盖封牢,外打铁箍加固,我们不反对用纸箱包装。

8. **plastic straps** 塑料箍,塑料带

   Please pack the Men's Shirts each inside a polythene bag, with a paper box outside, 100 boxes to a carton, bound with two plastic straps.

   请用纸盒包装男式衬衫,每件装一盒,内套一个聚乙烯塑料袋。一百盒装一纸箱,箱外打两道塑料带。

9. **be perforated with** 在……上钻孔

   This board is perforated with regularly spaced holes into which pegs can be fitted.

   这块板子上面均匀地凿有孔,这些孔可以插钉子。

10. **carton labels** 外箱贴纸

11. **perforated plate** 穿孔板

    原名冲孔板,就是在不同材质的板材上打孔,如不锈钢板、铝板、铁板、低碳钢板、铜板等。穿孔板在现实生活中的应用非常广泛,可作为装饰用板,美观大方。

12. **to be stenciled or printed with** 被印上……;刷唛

    Please stencil our initials and order number on the outer packing.

    请在外包装上印上我公司名称的首字母和订单号。

I. Translate the following expressions into Chinese or vice versa.

1. plastic straps   6. 可回收材料
2. 3-ply corrugated cardboard   7. 主唛
3. be sealed with   8. 用……加固
4. perforated plate   9. 包装须知
5. egg crate   10. 侧唛

II. Identify the one error in each of the following sentences.

(   ) 1. Pens are packed 24 pieces to a box and 200 boxes in a wooden case.
              A   B   C   D

(   ) 2. Styrol boxes are used to reducing weight, and they are so easy to carry.
                    A   B   C   D

(   ) 3. Our cartons for canned food are not only seaworth but also strong enough to
                          A   B   C
       protect the goods from possible damage.
                         D

(   ) 4. Since cartons are comparatively light and compact, they are more convenient
                              A   B
       to handle at the course of loading and unloading.
              C   D

(   ) 5. The boxes are packed in strong cardboard cartons, twelve for a carton, separated
                              A   B
       from each other by paper dividers.
         C   D

(   ) 6. The crates are lined with waterproof, airtight material. The lids are secured by
                              A   B   C
       nailing, and the crates are strapped in metal bands.
                                          D

III. Put the following into English.

1. 请刷上一菱形，内刷我公司名称首字母 ABC，其下应刷目的港及我方订单号。
2. 衬衣装在衬有塑料袋的纸箱里比装在木箱里不易受到潮损。
3. 12 双装一个外箱，外箱贴纸应该贴在外箱正唛头的一面，供应商信息如下。
4. 请确保箱子上标有"易碎品""小心搬运"的字样。
5. 经查，发现约有 10 袋未按合同规定以五层坚固纸袋包装，以致在运输途中造成破损。

IV. Translate sentences 10-15 in "Useful Expressions" for Chapter IX.

CHAPTER IX　PACKING & MARKING

Lesson 24

Container Loading

集装箱（container）又被称为"货柜"，是一种按规格标准化的钢制箱子。集装箱的特色在于其格式划一，可以层层重叠，所以可以大量放置于特别设计的远洋轮船上，为世界各地的生产商提供比空运更廉价的大量运输服务。集装箱船的大小一般以能装载多少 20 英尺标准箱（TEU, Twenty-feet Equivalent Units）计算，例如一个 40 英尺标准箱就是 2 TEU。

From: Jeremy Weiner @hotmail.com
To: alicia0618@tchina.com
Subject: container loading

Dear Alicia,

We experienced a high number of items delivered that were damaged and covered in mould. This resulted in lost sales and high costs in cleaning the products. We would ask you to monitor the following points on container loading and confirm back to us that these procedures are in place.

1. All PO's must be loaded separately. No mixing of PO's within a container is permitted.

Within each PO, goods must be sorted in size, so that in effect every order is segregated and consolidated. Each SKU must be loaded into the vehicle moving left to right, known as "snake loading".

2. If the bulk goods is not sufficient to fill the container in height and length, the goods should be "snake loaded" flat to fill up all length space, leaving spare volume at the top of the container. This helps to prevent collapsed loads whereby goods are loaded to fill height at rear of container, leaving space forward of the goods within the container.

3. Containers must NOT be overloaded as this risk damaging the cartons within.

4. Care should be taken to ensure bulk stock stay dry in packing and loading areas within the factory. Damp cartons can lead to mould found upon arrival.

5. All carton labels MUST be forward facing. If carton labels are mixed with some facing inwards, the bulks will be rejected.

6. Pallet loads are not acceptable.

We thank you for your co-operation in this matter.

Best regards,
Jeremy Weiner

1. **container loading** 装柜要求

    集装箱的种类有：杂货集装箱（Dry Container）、冷藏集装箱（Refrigerated Container）、散货集装箱（Solid Bulk Container）、开顶集装箱（Open Top Container）、框架集装箱（Flat Rack Container）、灌装集装箱（Tank Container）

2. **load** *v.* 装货，装载

    The steamer is loading for London. 该轮正在装货运往伦敦。

    load *n.* （一船）货物，装载量

    The goods ordered have been forwarded to you in three ship loads。

    所订货物分三次运往你方。

    loading *n.* 装货

    loading and unloading 装卸

    loading charges 装货费

    port of loading 装货港

3. **segregate** *v.* 分离；隔离

    segregate full and empty cylinders. 隔开满瓶和空瓶。

4. **snake loading** 蛇形装柜

    这是集装箱的一种装箱方法，就是"S"形装箱 先从集装箱最里面装，例如：第一排1—10箱，第二排就是20—11，第三排21—30……箱号顺序保持连续。主要是按照客人的意图，分色或分PO号或分码段，把纸箱连续逐段，有如长蛇似的装入集装箱；客人收到货柜后，也会按照相反的次序卸下纸箱，不会发生混乱。

5. **lead to** 导致

CHAPTER IX   PACKING & MARKING

6. "snake loaded" flat 平铺装柜

7. mould 发霉

8. forward facing 朝柜门装柜

9. pallet 货盘

拼装货物多装托盘便于搬运。托盘根据材料不同可分为木制托盘、塑料托盘、纸质托盘等。在目前国际贸易中，木制托盘使用较少，因为大多数国家要求对进口的木质材料熏蒸。

We have packed 168 boxes in 7 pallets of 24 boxes each.

我们已将 168 盒货物装于 7 个货盘，每个货盘装 24 盒。

I. Translate the following expressions into Chinese or vice versa.

1. carton labels
2. polybag
3. in good order
4. container
5. PO
6. 蛇形装柜
7. 装货费
8. 在运输途中
9. 货盘
10. 散货集装箱

II. Fill in the blanks with suitable prepositions.

1. All the canned fruits and meat are to be packed _____ cartons.
2. Our trip scissors are packed _____ boxes _____ 1 dozen each, 100 boxes _____ a carton lined _____ waterproof paper.
3. A thorough examination showed that the broken kegs were due _____ which the suppliers should be definitely responsible.
4. Pls see to it that the packing is suitable _____ a long sea voyage.
5. The tea _____ the captioned contract should be packed _____ international standard tea boxes, 24 boxes _____ a ballet, 10 pallets _____ an FCL container.
6. Please mark the outer packing _____ our initials SCC _____ a diamond, under which the port of destination and our order number should be stenciled.
7. We avail ourselves _____ this opportunity to assure you _____ our prompt

and careful attention _____ handling your further orders.

8. Pls pack the goods _____ small barrels, which must be lined _____ polythene.

III. Translate the following sentences into English.

1. 我们必须说明的是采用不同的包装材料，包装费用会不一样。
2. 茶叶应装国际标准茶叶盒，24盒装一托盘，10托盘装一整集装箱。
3. 所有的订单都要单独装柜，同一个柜子不允许装几个PO的货。
4. 考虑到货物的易碎性和昂贵的包装费用，请采用耐用包装和经济包装。
5. 在包装和装板条箱时，必须非常小心，因为在运输中的任何损坏将给我们造成严重损失。

Business Link

1. Some phrases concerning packing

packing mark	包装标志	packing design	包装设计
packing cost	包装成本	packing industry	包装业
packing test	包装试验	bulk packing	散装
vacuum packing	真空包装	sealed packing	密封包装
durable packing	耐用包装	economical packing	经济包装
packing free	免费包装	packing included	含包装费
neutral packing	中性包装	packing instructions	包装指示
packing list	包装单	packing method	包装方法
packing material	包装材料	unitary packing	个别包装
inner packing	内包装	outer packing	外包装
export packing	出口包装	seaworthy packing	适于海运的包装
packing clause	包装条款	delicate packing	精致的包装

2. Terms related to packing container

bag	袋，包	sack/gunny bag	麻袋
bale	包，布包	bundle	捆
box	盒，箱	carton	纸板箱
case	箱	wooden case	木箱

CHAPTER IX PACKING & MARKING

plywood case	三合板箱	crate	板条箱
cardboard cartons	纸板箱	iron case	铁箱
fiber board case	纤维板箱	cask	木桶
barrel	桶	drum	铁皮圆桶
keg	小圆桶	tin/can	听，罐
bomb/cylinder	钢桶	polythene bag	聚乙烯塑料袋
canvas bag	帆布袋	paper bag	纸袋

3. Some expressions concerning shipping marks

diamond	菱形	triangle	三角形
rectangle	长方形	square	正方形
heart	心形	circle	圆形
cross	十字形	star	星形
down triangle	倒三角形	oval	椭圆形
hexagon	正六角形	three diamond	三菱形

4. Special directions or warnings

此端向上（THIS SIDE UP）
顶端 （TOP）
易碎物品 （FRAGILE）
保持干燥（KEEP DRY）
避免日光直射（KEEP OUT OF THE DIRECT SUN）
危险品 （DANDEROUS GOODS）
禁止潮湿（GUARD AGAINST DAMP）
酸——小心 （ACID—WITH CARE）
请勿用钩 （USE NO HOOKS）
请勿平放（NOT TO BE LAID FLAT）
切勿坠落（DO NOT DROP）
切勿受热，隔离热气（KEEP AWAY FROM HEAT）
此端开启（OPEN THIS END）
低温存放，保持冷藏（TO KEEP COOL）
禁放甲板上（DO NOT STOW ON DECK）
小心搬运（HANDLE WITH CARE）
易燃物品 （INFLAMMABLE）
玻璃器皿——当心 （GLASSWARES—WITH CARE）

在此起吊 (LIFT HERE)
易腐物品 (PERISHABLE GOODS)

Skill Training

Exercise I. Write out the following packing containers.

CHAPTER IX   PACKING & MARKING

Exercise II. Design shipping marks and side marks according to the letter.

Dear Sirs,

PO No. Michael 423

In reply to your letter of the 31st August inquiring about the packing of our Trip Scissors, we wish to state as below:

Our export Trip Scissors are packed in boxes of one dozen each, 100 boxes to a carton. The dimensions are 17cm high, 30cm wide and 50cm long with a volume of about 0.026 cubic meter. The gross weight is 23.5kg while the net weight is 22.5kg. As to the shipping marks outside the carton, in addition to the gross, net weights and tare, the wording "MADE IN THE PEOPLE'S REPUBLIC OF CHINA" is also stenciled on the package. Port of destination is London, England. Should you have any special preference in this respect, please let us know and we will meet you to the best of our ability.

Taking this opportunity, we would like to inform you that we used to pack our scissors in wooden cases but after several trial shipments in carton packing, we found our cartons just as seaworthy as wooden cases. Besides, cartons are less expensive, lighter to carry and cost lower freight. So, nowadays more and more clients are preferring carton packing to wooden case packing. We trust that you will agree to our opinion and accept our carton packing.

We thank you in advance for your early reply.

Yours faithfully,
×××

Useful Expressions

1. The goods should be packed in a manner that ensures safe and sound arrival of goods at the destination and facilitates handling during transshipment.
2. Each carton is lined with a polythene sheet and secured by overall strapping, thus preventing the contents from dampness and possible damage through rough handling.

3. Please pack the socks each pair in a polybag, 12 dozen to a cardboard box, and 25 boxes to a carton.
4. Our packing is not only seaworthy but also strong enough to protect the goods from possible damage.
5. Our cotton prints are packed in cases lined with draft paper and waterproof paper, each consisting of 30 pieces in one design with 5 colourways equally assorted.
6. Our cartons for canned food are not only seaworthy but also strong enough to protect the goods from possible damage.
7. Please take necessary precautions that the packing can protect the goods from dampness or rain, since these goods are liable to be spoiled by damp or water in transit.
8. Please note that glass wares are fragile goods, so they need special packing precautions against jolting in transit.
9. 30 packets × 600 grams per wooden case or carton, each packet lined with white pater and outside wrapped up in cellophane paper, 2% more or less in weight for each case allowed.
10. In fact, this packing is both shockproof and waterproof. Nevertheless we have still marked the cartons with warnings like "THIS SIDE UP", "HANDLE WITH CARE", "FRAGILE" and "USE NO HOOKS".
11. In order to avoid the fungus problem for any of our merchandise, please pay your special attention and make sure that all the merchandise are totally dried before packing.
12. The goods have been packed and marked exactly as directed so that they may be shipped by the first ship available towards the end of this month.
13. We trust that you will give special care to the packing in order to avoid damage in transit.
14. Please let us have your shipping advice by fax immediately stating the name of vessel so that we may effect insurance at this end.
15. Shipment is to be made during May to July in three equal lots.

CHAPTER X
SHIPMENT

Objectives:

After learning this chapter, you will

1. be familiar with some trade terms and terminologies on shipping.
2. be familiar with the procedure of arranging the shipment.
3. be able to write letters on shipment.

Introduction

装运是指卖方按合同履行交货的义务。FOB，CIF，CFR 都是"装运港交货"的贸易术语。卖方把货物在装运港装上轮船，取得货运单据并交给买方，即可作为履行交货。因此对这三种合同，人们常把"交货"的概念和"装运"等同起来。据此，交易条件中的"交货条件"也可称为"装运条件"。

在对外贸易中，合同的装运条件十分重要，它涉及装运时间、装运港、目的港、运输方式和货运单据等。装运时间一般是规定一个期限，而不是某个肯定的具体日期。装运港是指货物的启运港。目的港则指货物被最终运达的目的地，一般由买方根据使用和销售需要提出，经卖方同意确定。运输方式根据运输工具的不同可分为海洋、铁路、航空和邮包运输、联合运输等。在各种提单中，班轮提单比较常用，是重要的单据。

把握装运的第一程序，安排好装运的各个环节，检查各种装运单证是否齐全并及时与买方沟通有关情况等，是装运函电的主要内容，卖方能否最终取得货款，买方能否最终收取货物，关键都在于装运的圆满完成。重视装运工作，及时拟制装运函电，是不能有半点疏忽的。因面对情况复杂，不可预知因素经常发生，装运函电拟写者需要审时度势，知人知己，巧妙运畴于书信之中，这是必不可少的。

有关装运的信函通常涉及以下几个方面：装运指示、装运通知、催促早日装运、修改装运条款、关于分批和装运的要求、装运单据等。

Writing Strategy

装运须知信函的写作步骤如下：
1. 提及货物、订单号等。
2. 告知卖方货代联系方式、装运方式和订舱时间等。
3. 对装运过程（拍照片、录像）的要求。
4. 感谢合作。

催促/允许分批或转运函的写作步骤如下：
1. 提及该货。
2. 告知催促（销售季节、季节性货物、货物畅销或卖方没有按时交货）/允许分批或转运（买方急需货物、工厂生产能力、无舱位）的理由。
3. 感谢合作。

Lesson 25

(A) Shipping Instructions

装运前买方将装运要求以书面形式通知卖方洽办，说明装船方式、包装规定和唛头等，称为"装运须知"（Shipping Instructions）。装船通知也叫装运通知（Shipping Advice），主要指的是出口商在货物装船后发给进口商的包括货物详细装运情况的通知，其目的在于让进口商做好筹措资金、付款和接货的准备。为了确保万无一失，买方要求供货方拍照片或录像显示装货和铅封全过程及集装箱和铅封号码。

From: Jeremy Weiner
To: Alicia
Subject: forwarder information

Dear Alicia,

Thank you very much for your information covering the readiness of our goods under Order No. HP2009029. Please contact our forwarder—NYK for shipment. NYK only handles CY (or FCL) in Xiamen port. LCL shipment (less container line) should be shipped to Hong Kong (Yantian or Shenzhen port).

CHAPTER X SHIPMENT

Contact person: Wen Shuen—Guangdong, China
Phone: 86-755-75757575 (Mr. Wang or Mrs. Wang)
Fax: 86-755-75863176
Email: wenshuen@ms37.hinet.net

Please make the order stated with the correct FOB point, depending on whether it's LCL or FCL cargo.

Booking must be done 14 days prior to shipping to ensure the shipping space. Late booking will result in US$350.00 charge back. Please surrender the original BL to shipping agent to make telex release to allow us to make clearance of the goods right away as the storage fee is $300.00 per day.

For full container shipments loaded by the factory, A.B.S has requested that before container leaves the factory, photos or video clip MUST be taken to show enough full quantity of the merchandise which has been packed and sealed into the container properly.

Please also note that the factory must take pictures once seal lock bar is installed and maintain records. The photos need to include both seal lock numbers and container numbers clear to read. A compliance charge of US$150.00 will be charged to those who don't document seal procedures.

Thank you in advance for your cooperation.

Best regards,
Jeremy Weiner

(B) A Reply

From: Alicia
To: Jeremy Weiner
Sent: 27 Oct., 2010 10: 07 AM
Subject: forwarder information

Dear Jeremy Weiner,

Thanks for your kind information about forwarder. I have contacted her accordingly.

As contracted, we will receive the balance first, and then release cargo by telex. We are waiting for your bank receipt. Here is revised PI and other shipping DOCs for your confirmation, including CI, CO, PL and BL. Please advise back soon.

Thank you for your attention.

Best regards,
Alicia

1. **CY（Container Yard）** 集装箱（货柜）堆场，实际操作上，CY 一般代表整箱装运，而 CFS（Container Freight Station）代表拼箱装运。
   FCL（Full Container Load，整箱）是指货方自行将货物装满整箱以后，以箱为单位托运的集装箱。
   LCL（Less than Container Load，拼箱）是指承运人（或代理人）接受货主托运的数量不足整箱的小票货运后，根据货类性质和目的地进行分类整理。把去同一目的地的货，集中到一定数量拼装入箱。由于一个箱内有不同货主的货拼装在一起，所以叫拼箱。

2. **book shipping space**
   shipping space broker 舱位经纪人
   congestion of shipping space 舱位拥挤
   Subject to shipping space available 以有舱位为准

3. **prior to** 在……之前
   Please open the L/C one month prior to the shipment. 请在装运一个月前开出信用证。
   Please try your best to ship one third of the goods prior to the shipment.
   请尽量能在装运前发运三分之一的货物。

4. **NYK (Nippon Yusen Kaisha)** 日本邮船株式会社，是日本三大海运公司之一，从事集装箱运输服务以及其他相关运输业务和物流服务，从成立至今已有一百多年的历史，其规模和业务量在世界航运企业中排名前列。
5. **storage fee** 仓储费

    还有：demurrage charges（车、船）滞期费，dead freight 空舱费。
6. **seal lock number** 铅封号

    货物装好之后，给集装箱上一个"锁"，其实是铅封，每个铅封上面都有一个号码，铅封只有破坏才可以打开。集装箱装运，提单上应注明装载货物的集装箱号，通常在集装箱号之后还加注海关查验后作为封箱的铅制关封号。如果是集装箱提单，应将这些内容填入专门设置的集装箱号铅封号栏。如果是其他类型的提单，可随意填在提单空白处。
7. **telex release** 电放，指的是海上货物承运人或者其装货港代理在收到货物签发或应该签发而未签发提单后，根据托运人要求在装货港收回提单或不签发正本提单，以电传形式通知卸货港代理将货物交付给提单收货人或者是托运人指定的收货人的一种方式。
8. **bank receipt** 银行付款回执单（银行水单）。T/T 付款在一般情况下，3 个工作日即可入账。在客户转账后，通常都会要求客户提供银行水单。
9. **DOCs** 即 documents。如果是信用证付款，信用证上会明确陈述所有关于出货的细节。如果不是信用证付款，在出货之前，必须向客户了解并核实出货的细节要求。因为这些文件关系到客户在当地是否可以出关，或者是否容易出关。

    出货后需要提交 packing list/commercial invoice/BL。

    BL（Bill of Lading）或 B/L，即"Marine Bill of Lading"或"Ocean Bill of Lading"，是指用以证明海上货物运输合同和货物已经由承运人接收或者装船，以及承运人保证据以交付货物的单证。相关的表达用语有：

    DIRECT B/L 直达提单，THROUGH B/L 联运提单或称转船提单

    MT B/L 多式联运提单，STRAIGHT B/L 记名提单

    CLEAN B/L 清洁提单，FOUL B/L 不清洁提单，ANTI-DATED B/L 倒签提单

    CO=certificate of origin 货物原产地

    CI=commercial invoice 出货之前要做的商业发票

    PL=packing list 出货之前要做的装箱单

Exercises

I. Translate the following expressions into Chinese or vice versa.

1. shipping instructions
2. prior to
3. bank receipt
4. FCL
5. seal lock numbers
6. 舱位拥挤
7. 电放
8. 唛头
9. 仓储费
10. 导致

II. Complete the following sentences in English.

1. Thank you very much for your information _____ （关于483号订单项下货物备妥的消息）.

2. Please _____（联系我们的货代——马士基航运公司安排装运）.

3. _____（订舱）must be done _____（装运期前14天进行以确保舱位）.

4. Photos must be taken to show enough _____（全部商品数量）which _____（被包装并打封入集装箱）properly.

5. We have pleasure in informing you that we have completed the shipment _____ （根据第KH40483NR款的规定）.

III. Translate the following sentences into English.

1. 我们会订一个40尺整柜，剩下的部分就走散货。
2. 麻烦你让货代安排另一班快船。
3. 集装箱铅封号分别是C417195和C417197。
4. 请注意柜子离开工厂之前，工厂必须保证柜门是封锁的，拍照留底为证。
5. 再次检验将导致1000美元的额外费用。

CHAPTER X SHIPMENT

Lesson 26

(A) Confirming Delivery Date (1)

及时交货是合同的一项规定。由于销售季节、季节性货物或货物畅销等因素影响，买方会催促卖方及时交货，而卖方由于货物排期紧张、办理海关手续、货代爆仓或甩柜等原因延误船期需及时向买方解释并获得买方确认。

From: Benjamin
To: Roy
Subject: prompt shipment

Hi Roy,

Our current production is fully booked. We really have difficulty squeezing this order in. If you insist on Feb. 1 delivery, we may have to find a subcontractor to make these hikers.

We do not want subcontracting because we cannot guarantee quality from other factory.

Our production is booked up to Apr. 15, 2010.
Therefore we hope you can accept our earliest delivery Mar. 30, 2010 to ensure good quality.

Pls confirm & comment.

Best regards,
Benjamin

(B) Confirming Delivery Date (2)

From: Benjamin

To: Mercy

Subject: prompt shipment

Dear Mercy,

Thanks for your mail. My daughter is 13 month and she is learning to walk. She likes reading picture books. You can see that from the photo attached.

I did talk to Roy. After our conversation with Roy, we did re-work on our production schedule (that was Ada's yesterday mail). Actually we worry about March 30 delivery. It may be too tight for our production. Because the orders we got (from October to April) were already 10% more than our production capacity.

Delivery time from our Production dept. is April 15.

Ada keeps pushing them for earlier delivery. We are planning to expand our factory after CNY. March 30 is really our earliest delivery.

Pls review and confirm.

Best regards,
Benjamin

1. **squeeze** *vt. & vi.* 挤，榨，捏；压迫，压榨

    We cannot borrow money during the present credits' squeeze.
    在银根紧的时候，我们借不出钱来。

    We managed to squeeze for you one shipment of Daqing crude in 10,000 metric tons, when we have been committed with orders from our regular customers.
    虽然我们把货都卖给了老客户，我们还是设法给你拿到了一批一万公吨的大庆原油。

CHAPTER X　SHIPMENT

2. **subcontractor** *n.* 转包工作的承包者，分包者，转包人

   We can contract to build turn-key plant, undertake single items of projects as a subcontractor or provide labor services.
   我们可以承建成套工厂或分包单项工程或提供劳务。
   We do not accept subcontracting of test to qualified subcontractor of SGS-CSTC.
   本公司不接受把样品交予其他具备资格的分包公司作检测。
   The manufacture of belts and buckles is put out to subcontractor.
   成带和带扣的生产交分包商承做。

3. **hiker** *n.* 远足者，长途旅行者，在这里指慢跑运动鞋或登山运动鞋

4. **ensure** *vt.* 担保；保证；使安全；确保

   These arrangements would ensure them a reasonable income.
   这些安排会保证他们得到合理的收入。
   Ensure that it is written into your contract. 请确保把这一点写入合同中。
   Please ensure you have read the terms and conditions.
   请确保您已阅读本条款和条件。

5. **CNY** 中国新年（Chinese New Year）的缩写

I. Translate the following expressions into Chinese or vice versa.

1. subcontractor　　　　　　6. 记名提单
2. production schedule　　　　7. 订舱位
3. container yard　　　　　　8. 清关
4. CNY　　　　　　　　　　9. 商业发票
5. production capacity　　　　10. 导致

II. Translate the following letter into Chinese and then write a reply to this letter.

Dear Sirs,

Contract No. CT110

Referring to our Order No. CT110 for 3,000 intellectual toys, we wish to call your attention to the fact that the shipment is approaching, nothing has been received from you about its shipment under the captioned contract.

We stated explicitly at the time of placing the order the importance of punctual shipment, your delay in shipment has put us to too much trouble and we must now ask you to do your utmost to dispatch the goods in question without delay, as our customers urgently require the goods.

We await your early reply.

Yours faithfully,
×××

III. Translate the following sentences into English.
1. 春节前由于处于旺季及劳力短缺，把交货期推迟到3月30日，这是我们的责任。
2. 我们会安排货物空运，并承担运费。
3. 我们计划空运货物30%，另外70%走海运。
4. 我们会扩大生产规模来确保质量。
5. 根据合同要求，货物装运后我们立即寄出全套不可转让的副本单据。
6. 已经强调货物必须在规定时间内装运，我方不考虑进一步展期。

Lesson 27

Asking for Partial Shipment

在传递不好的消息时，写作策略很重要的一点是解释原因并提出补救措施。在本案例里，卖方实事求是地解释原因，因为这些情况的发生是正常的，从头到尾没有一句 sorry，但是却可以感受到卖方认真诚恳的态度。订单延期补救的方法有分批装运、空运部分货物以及赔偿延误天数的损失。

From: Winnie
To: Eva
Re: CZ, Russia & Hungary Order (Total 3 × 40'GP and 1 × 40'HQ containers)

Dear Eva,

We planned to delivery all the goods under CZ, Russia and Hungary to catch vessel of Aug. 12, 2018.

CHAPTER X SHIPMENT

However, unfortunately, for style # 506.DD & 506.DD LADY, when the outsole of these styles delivered to our warehouse yesterday, we found most of the outsoles for these 2 styles have problems, the black color on the outsole are split. We always want to make the good shoes for all customers; especially for Head brand, which is a worldwide brand. To guarantee the shoe quality, we returned these inferior outsoles to suppliers and requested them to remake them, and the remade outsoles will be finished around on Aug. 12.

In this sudden case, some of the goods under CZ, Russia and Hungary will be rushed & finished around on Aug. 14 when the remade outsoles arrive.

So we suggest to ship first 2 × 40'GP containers (details as 1st sheet in the attached form), and the second 1 × 40'HQ & 1 × 40'GP containers (details as 2nd sheet in the attached form) will catch the next vessel on Aug. 19. Kindly review & comment ASAP. We will highly appreciate it if you can confirm to us today, so we can update the booking with forwarder. Thank you in advance.

Look forward to your immediate reply.

Thanks & best regards,
Winnie
(CC: Mr. Danny Chan)

1. **partial shipments** 分批装运
   指一个合同项下的货物分若干批或若干期装运。
2. **3 × 40'GP and 1 × 40'HQ** 3 个 40 英尺普柜，1 个 40 英尺高柜
   另外还有 20'GP, 40'GP 等柜型。
3. **warehouse** *n.* 仓库
   warehouse to warehouse clause 仓至仓条款
   We adopt the warehouse to warehouse clause that is commonly used in international insurance. 我们采用国际保险中常用的"仓至仓"责任条款。

Our warehouse is located in Illinois. Could you please provide us door to door service?

我们的仓库在（美国）伊利诺伊州。你们能不能为我们提供门到门服务？

4. **Head brand** "海德"牌

奥地利著名运动品牌，主打滑雪用品，产品覆盖滑雪、健身、网球、游泳、潜水等多个领域。

5. **guarantee** *vt.* 保证，担保

Please inform us whether you can guarantee your products.

请告知贵公司是否愿意对产品加以保证。

6. **inferior** *adj.* （质量等）低劣的；下级的，下等的

The quality of your products is inferior to the goods of French origin.

你们的产品质量比法国产的差。

I. Translate the following expressions into Chinese or vice versa.

1. port of loading   6. 订舱位
2. GP   7. 仓至仓条款
3. freight collect   8. 转运
4. vessel name   9. 预订集装箱
5. congestion of shipping space   10. 班轮运输

II. Fill in the blanks with proper prepositions.

1. Please ship the first lot _____ Contract No. 512 _____ S.S. Dongfeng, scheduled to sail _____ or about 5th November.

2. We hope that the goods can be shipped _____ two equal monthly installments of 3,000 sets each.

3. The factory should book _____ the forwarder 14 days _____ DCD date. If any factory fails to comply _____ this requirement, factory will be charged back USD500 _____ non-compliance.

4. As there is no direct steamer, shipment has to be transshipped _____ Hong Kong.

5. We are glad to inform you that we have shipped your goods _____ S.S. "Peace" which is due to leave tomorrow.

CHAPTER X　SHIPMENT

III. Translate the following sentences into English.
1. 因港口拥挤，很多货物不得不在鹿特丹转船。
2. 我们借此通知你方我们已经把上述货物装到维多利亚轮上，该船于明天驶往你港。
3. 第 2048 号订单的货物 70% 在 11 月装运，其余在 12 月装运。
4. 一万公吨大豆因舱位不够，无法全部在 10 月份装运，请修改信用证，允许分批装运。
5. 由于你方要求提前装运，额外的运费由买方承担。

Business Link

1. 海运出口货物流程
1) 订舱并填写订舱单：出口商根据合同中的最迟装运时间，提前 8—10 个工作日向货运代理公司订舱。
2) 货运公司确认了出口商的订舱后，出口商即可获得出口运输方面最重要的信息：船公司的名称、航班号、转船时间、开船时间、预计到达目的港的天数。
3) 获得场站收据：货运公司把货物运到装运港集装箱码头堆场后方，货运公司获得场站收据，转交给出口商，以便出口商自行报检和报关。
4) 准备装船：出口货物通过报检和报关后，把有关单据交给货运公司，货运公司则将有关单据交给场站工作人员，工作人员把集装箱运到集装箱码头堆场前方，等待装船。
5) 装船并获得海运提单：场站工作人员根据集装箱的转船时间（此时间写在订舱单上）装船。装船后，货运公司从船公司获得海运提单。
6) 支付海运费：出口商支付海运费，货运公司把海运提单交给出口商。
7) 出口商向进口商发送装船通知。

2. 船务术语简写
1) ORC (Origin Receive Charges) 本地收货费用
2) THC (Terminal Handling Charges) 码头操作费
3) BAF (Bunker Adjustment Factor) 燃油附加费
4) CAF (Currency Adjustment Factor) 货币贬值附加费
5) YAS (Yard Surcharges) 码头附加费
6) EPS (Equipment Position Surcharges) 设备位置附加费

7) DDC (Destination Delivery Charges) 目的港交货费

8) PSS (Peak Season Surcharges) 旺季附加费

9) PCS (Port Congestion Surcharge) 港口拥挤附加费

10) DOC (Document Charges) 文件费

11) O/F (Ocean Freight) 海运费

12) B/L (Bill of Lading) 海运提单

13) MB/L (Master Bill of Lading) 船东单

14) MTD (Multimodal Transport Document) 多式联运单据

15) W/T (Weight Ton) 重量吨（即货物收费以重量计费）

16) M/T (Measurement Ton) 尺码吨（即货物收费以尺码计费）

17) W/M (Weight or Measurement Ton) 即以重量吨或者尺码吨中从高收费

18) CY (Container Yard) 集装箱（货柜）堆场

19) FCL (Full Container Load) 整箱货

20) LCL (Less than Container Load) 拼箱货（散货）

21) CFS (Container Freight Station) 集装箱货运站

22) TEU (Twenty-feet Equivalent Units) 20 英尺换算单位（用来计算货柜量的多少）

23) A/W (All Water) 全水路（指由美国西岸中转至东岸或内陆点的货物的运输方式）

24) MLB (Mini Land Bridge) 迷你大陆桥（主要指由美国西岸中转至东岸或内陆点的货物的运输方式）

3. 货运英语名词总汇

定期租船 time charter

允许装卸时间 lay days || laying days

工作日 working days

连续天数 running days || consecutive days

滞期费 demurrage

滞期日数 demurrage days

速遣费 despatch money

空舱费 dead freight

退关 short shipment || goods short shipped || goods shut out || shut-outs

赔偿保证书（信托收据）letter of indemnity || trust receipt

装运重量 shipping weight || in-take-weight

卸货重量 landing weight

压舱 ballasting

压舱货 in ballast

CHAPTER X SHIPMENT

舱单 manifest
船舶登记证书 ship's certificate of registry
航海日记 ship's log
船员名册 muster-roll
（船员、乘客的）健康证明 bill of health

Skill Training

Exercise I. Fill in the blanks with the hints below.

装货港：福建福州
提单号：DDC123456
集装箱铅封号：GATU12345/65432
预计到达时间：2021年1月20日
货物名称：时尚拖
总重量：3000KGS
净重：2340KGS
数量：5200双
总金额：21645.12美元
开证行：the Banca Monte Dei Paschi Di Siena S.p.A.
唛头：A.B.S/C number—order number—art. number   port of destination: CATANIA

发票号码：HJ20100098
船名：VICTORY NO. 345P
装运日期：2020年12月30日
签发日期：2021年1月2日
合同号码：BP12345
信用证号码：HS84283AF
通知日期：2020年12月30日
目的港：CATANIA PORT, ITALY

FUJIAN ORIENTAL FOOTWEAR IMP. AND EXP. CO., LTD.		
Add: 9/F MINFA BUILDING NO. 88, DONGSHUI ROAD, FUZHOU, CHINA		
Tel: 86-591-34567890 Mobile: 86-12345678900		
Web: www.orientalfootwear.com Email: alicia0618@tchina.com		
SHIPPING ADVICE		
TO: AL ABRA SUB TRADING EST. 94017 REGALBUTO CATANIA, ITALY	ISSUE DATE:	
	S/C NO.:	
	L/C NO.:	
	DATE:	
	NAME OF ISSUING BANK:	

Dear Sir or Madam:

We have pleasure in informing you that we have completed the shipment in accordance with the stipulations set forth in L/C No. HS84283AF. The details of shipment are stated below:

Invoice Number:	
Bill of Loading Number:	
Ocean Vessel:	
Port of Loading:	
Date of Shipment:	
Port of Destination:	
ETA	
Containers/Seals Number:	
Description of Goods:	
Shipping Marks:	
Quantity:	
Gross Weight:	
Net Weight:	
Total Value:	

Thank you for your patronage. We look forward to the pleasure of receiving your valuable repeat orders.

Sincerely yours,

FOR AND ON BEHALF OF:

FUJIAN ORIENTAL FOOTWEAR IMP. AND EXP. CO., LTD.

Alicia

Exercise II. Put the following letter into English.

执事先生：

我方近期内将有20箱瓷器（chinaware）从香港运往鹿特丹（Rotterdam），货箱尺码为5英尺×4英尺×3英尺，每箱重约250公斤。

请告知货物运价，以及航运班期、运货所需要的时间等详细情况。据悉"恒星"号轮定于8月10日启航，但我方希望有启航日期较早的货轮。

盼早复。

谨启

CHAPTER X SHIPMENT

Useful Expressions

1. Please be assured that we will effect shipment in compliance with the contracted terms.
2. However, up to now we have not received from you any information concerning this lot.
3. As the selling season is rapidly approaching, we shall appreciate it very much if you will book shipping space and arrange shipment as soon as possible, thus enable the goods to catch the brisk demand at the start of the season.
4. Enclosed please find one set of duplicate shipping documents for the goods, the original of which are being sent to you through our bankers.
5. We take pleasure in notifying you that the consignment under S/C No. 409 have been made on board S.S. Victoria which is sailing from Hong Kong to New York via Panama Canal on July 20 and is due to arrive at New York on or about Aug. 8.
6. We have to advise you that we are unable to dispatch your order in full owing to a great shortage of shipping space.
7. The goods ordered in May are ready for dispatch and as the transaction is concluded on FOB basis you are to arrange the shipment. We should be glad to have your immediate shipping instructions.
8. The ETS would be two weeks after receipt of order. However, with the port workers now on strike, we doubt it if we could make shipment in time. We assure you that we are doing everything we can to get the goods away.
9. Please advise us 30 days before the month of shipment of the contract number, name of commodity, quantity, port of loading and the time when the goods reach the port of loading.
10. Much to our regret, we cannot ship the goods within the time limit of the L/C owing to the unforeseen difficulties on the part of mill.
11. The duplicate shipping documents including bill of lading, invoice, packing list and inspection certificate were airmailed to you today.
12. In the event of force majeure or any contingencies beyond our control, we shall not be held responsible for the late delivery or non-delivery of the goods.
13. We hope you will understand that we would not ask for earlier delivery if we did not have compelling reasons for doing so.

14. The shipment must be made within the prescribed time limit, as further extension will not be considered.
15. As our traditional Spring Festival holiday is approaching, it will be very difficult for us to book shipping space. To make it easier, we hope transshipment and partial shipments are allowed.

CHAPTER XI
INSURANCE

Objectives:
After learning this chapter, you will
1. be familiar with some terms related to insurance.
2. be familiar with insurance policies.
3. be able to write letters on insurance.

Introduction

在国际贸易中，货物从卖方到买方手中，通常要经过长途的运输、装卸和存储等流转环节，在这个过程中货物可能会遇到自然灾害或意外事故而遭受各种损失。为了货物受损时能得到经济上的补偿，买方或卖方应在货物装运前联系保险公司办理货物的运输保险。

所谓货物的运输保险是指投保人（the insured，在 FOB，CFR 术语下为买方，在 CIF 术语下为卖方）对一批或若干批货物向保险人（the insurer，即保险公司），按一定的保险金额（insurance amount）投保一定的险别（coverage），并缴纳保险费（premium）；保险人承保后签发保险单（insurance policy）作为承保的保险凭证（insurance certificate）。

保险金额是保险公司对责任范围内的损失进行赔偿的最高金额，一般按 CIF 或 CIP 的总值加 10% 确定，必要时也可超过 10%。险别是确定承保人赔偿的责任范围，不同的险别承保人承担的责任范围是不同的。保险单和保险凭证是保险合同的书面证明。在保险合同生效后，承保人就要负责对投保货物在运输过程中遭受的所保险别保险责任范围的损失，按投保金额及损失程度赔偿给被保险人。这不仅有利于进出口企业加强经济核算，而且也有利于进出口企业保持正常营业，从而有效地促进国际贸易的发展。

在本章节中，我们向学生介绍在对外贸易中常见的保险条款及保险险别。

Writing Tips

卖方保险信函的写法如下：

1. 说明收到信函，指出所订的货品已安排装运。

2. 确认对方要求办理保险，告知对方投标险别、保险条款、保险单据及列出投保金额。

3. 希望对方同意。

买方保险信函的写法如下：

1. 提示合同、货物等。

2. 提出具体保险要求及理由。

3. 希望对方同意并尽早发货。

Lesson 28

Insurance Information

出口货物如按 CIF 和 CIP 成交，应由出口企业向当地中国人民财产保险股份有限公司（PICC P&C，简称"中国人保财险"）办理投保手续。如买方要求按照海洋运输货物保险条款投保，则所产生的额外保费由买方承担。

From: Angela@timbag.com

To: jan@busytrade.co.nz

Subject: information on our insurance terms

Dear Jan,

In reply to your email of last Friday enquiring about the insurance on our CIF offer for QX-508 Leather Bag, we wish to give you the following information.

For transactions concluded on CIF basis, we usually effect insurance with the People's Insurance Company of China against All Risks, as per Ocean Marine Cargo Clauses of the People's Insurance Company of China, dated the 1st January, 1981. Should you require the insurance to be covered as per Institute Cargo Clauses we would be glad to comply but if there is any difference in premium between the two, it will be charged to your account.

We are also in a position to insure the shipment against any additional risks if you so desire, and the extra premium is to be borne by you. In this case, we shall send you the premium receipt issued by the relative underwriter.

Looking forward to receiving your order.

Best regards,
Angela

1. **insurance** *n.* 保险

    effect/cover/provide/take out insurance 投保

    insurance amount 保险金额

    insurance policy 保单

    insurance certificate 保险凭证

    insurance coverage 保险范围

    Insurance is to be covered by the sellers for 110% of the invoice value.
    由卖方以发票价值 110% 投保。
    表示投保的货物，后接 on；表示保险金额，后接 for；表示投保的险别，后接 against；表示保险费或保险费率，后接 at；表示向保险公司投保，后接 with。例如：
    We have covered insurance on the 5000 sets "LENOVO" Brand Computer for 110% of the invoice value against All Risks and War Risk with the PICC P&C.
    我们已将 5000 台"联想"牌电脑按发票金额的 110% 向中国人保财险投保一切险。
    insure *v.* 投保；承保
    We will insure the shipment with the People's Insurance Company of China.
    我们将向中国人保为这票货投保。
    What risks are to be insured against? 要投什么险？

insurer *n.* 承保人，保险人

the insured 投保人

2. People's Insurance Company of China 中国人民保险公司

中国人民保险公司成立于1949年，现更名为中国人民保险集团股份有限公司［People's Insurance Company (Group) of China Limited］，旗下包含中国人民财产保险股份有限公司、中国人民人寿保险股份有限公司等。本书按照行业邮件的习惯用法，以 People's Insurance Company of China 指代中国人民财产保险股份有限公司。中国人民保险公司于1981年1月1日制定的中国保险条款（China Insurance Clauses，缩写为 C.I.C. 或 CIC），包括海洋（Ocean Marine Cargo Insurance）、陆上（Overland Transportation）、航空（Air Transportation）及邮包（Parcel Transportation）运输方式的货物运输保险条款，以及适用于以上四种运输方式货物保险的附加条款。

3. Ocean Marine Cargo 海洋运输货物保险

海洋运输货物保险分为基本险和附加险两类。基本险所承保的主要是自然灾害和意外事故所造成的货物损失与费用，分为平安险（Free from Particular Average，简称 FPA）、水渍险（with Average 或 with Particular Average，简称 WA 或 WPA）和一切险（All Risks，简称 AR）三种。附加险（Extraneous Risks）是对基本险的补充和扩大，附加险只能在投保某一种基本险的基础上才可加保。附加险有一般附加险（Additional Risks）和特殊附加险（Special Additional Risks）之分。

4. Institute Cargo Clauses 伦敦保险协会制定的货物保险条款

该条款共包括六种险别：(1) 协会货物条款 (A)［Institute Cargo Clause A，简称 ICC(A)］；(2) 协会货物条款 (B)［简称 ICC(B)］；(3) 协会货物条款 (C)［简称 ICC(C)］；(4) 协会战争险条款（货物）（Institute War Clause-Cargo）；(5) 协会罢工险条款（货物）（Institute Strikes Clause-Cargo）；(6) 恶意损坏条款（Malicious Damage Clause）。

5. account *n.* 账户

take account of sth./take sth. into account 考虑，注意到

They should have taken into account the need of foreign customers.

他们应该考虑到海外客户的需求。

settle your account 付账，结账

Accounts must be settled within 30 days.

必须在30天内结账。

on account of 因为，由于

CHAPTER XI INSURANCE

The shipment is delayed on account of the late arrival of some raw materials.

account for 占有；解释

Oil and gas accounts for 60% of the country's export.

石油和天热气占到这个国家出口的 60%。

How do you account for the sudden change of export regulations?

你如何解释出口规定的突然变化？

6. be in a position to 能够

We are not in a position to take on new business at present. 目前我们不能开展新的业务。

7. insurance premium 保险费

8. underwriter *n.* 保险商

underwriter 与 insurance company 与 insurer 一般可以通用，但 underwriter 主要指专保水险的保险商。

The underwriters suggest the buyer insure all risks. 保险商建议买方投一切险。

underwrite *v.* 保险

Insurers here will not underwrite this risk. 这儿的投保人将不投这种险别。

Exercises

I. Translate the following expressions into Chinese or vice versa.

1. All Risks
2. Institute Cargo Clauses
3. additional risks
4. C.I.C.
5. be charged to your account
6. 以 CIF 价格成交
7. 向中国人保财险投保
8. 承担额外的保费
9. 保费收据
10. 为这票货投保

II. Choose the best answer.

(　　) 1. I'd like to have the insurance _____ for 130% of the invoice value.

　　A. cover　　　B. covered　　　C. covering　　　D. to cover

(   ) 2. We are pleased to confirm _____ the above goods against All Risks for $5,500.
   A. have arranged   B. having assured
   C. to have ensured   D. having insured

(   ) 3. We thank you for your letter of March 25, requesting us to effect insurance on the captioned goods for your _____.
   A. cost   B. amount   C. account   D. expense

(   ) 4. Since the premium varies with the extent of insurance, extra premium is borne by the buyer, _____ additional risks be covered.
   A. if   B. as   C. must   D. should

(   ) 5. Insurance _____ will be added to invoice amount together with the freight charges.
   A. policies   B. premiums   C. money   D. amount

III. Translate the following sentences into English.

1. 我们是按 FOB 价达成交易的，所以由你方去投保。
2. 对于按 CIF 价成交的货物，由我方按发票金额的 110% 投保一切险。
3. 因为这批货不是易碎品，不太可能在运输途中受损，所以平安险就够了。
4. 破碎险是一种特殊险别，要额外收保费。
5. 由于保险费率随保险范围而不同，因此如需增报其他险别，额外保费由买方负担。

Lesson 29

Insurance Clause

保险单上的条文规定了有关保险人与被保险人的权利、义务及其他保险事项。保险单上都印有保险条款，中国海洋运输货物保险条款是中国人民保险公司参照国际通常做法结合我国实际情况拟定的，经过几十年来的应用与实践，已被国际贸易、航运、保险界广泛接受。

CHAPTER XI INSURANCE

From: Amy@genway.com
To: Scott@paemaesales.com
Date: Aug. 5, 2020 11:49
Subject: additional risk of breakage

Dear Scott,

We refer to your L/C No. 1210 regarding Porcelains, which we have just received.

Please note that we do not cover Breakage for this cargo. Therefore you have to delete the word "Breakage" from the insurance clause in the letter of credit.

Moreover, we'd like to stress that Breakage is a special risk. For such goods as Window Glass, Glazed Wall Tiles, etc. even if Additional Risk of Breakage has been insured, the cover is subject to a franchise of 5%. That is to say, if the breakage is surveyed to be less than 5%, no claims for damage will be entertained.

We trust that everything is now clear. Please amend your L/C by telex ASAP.

Best regards,
Amy

1. **cover** *v.* 保险，投保
   We shall cover the goods against war risk. 我们将此货物投保战争险。
   We shall cover FPA for you. 我们将为你代办投保平安险。
   Buyers will cover insurance on the captioned goods. 买方为标题项下的商品投保。
   The insurance policy covers us against breakage. 保险单给我们保破碎险。
   cover *n.* 保险
   insurance cover 保险
   We have arranged the necessary insurance cover. 我们已经投了必要的保险。
   coverable *adj.* 可投保的，可承保的
   Breakage Risk is coverable for the goods. 此商品的破碎险是可投保的。

2. **moreover** 此外（相当于 besides, in addition, furthermore）
   Moreover/Besides/In addition/Furthermore we are on good terms with the ABC Insurance Company. 此外我们与 ABC 保险公司关系良好。

3. **Glazed Wall Tiles** 釉面砖

4. **franchise** *n.* 免赔率（额）；特权，特许
   These articles are sold with a franchise of 3%. 这些商品按照百分之三的免赔率出售。
   We have received a franchise from the government to deal with this kind of business.
   我们已经从政府那里得到特权去处理这种生意。

5. **survey** *v.* 调查，检查，观察，鉴定
   survey report 调查报告，检验报告
   Please survey the market conditions of the new products. 请调查新产品的市场情况。
   Please survey the situation closely and keep us informed of the developments.
   请密切观察情况并随时告诉我们发展状况。
   Please make a detailed survey of the market conditions of the new products.
   请对新产品的市场情况做一份详细的调查。

I. Translate the following expressions into Chinese or vice versa.

1. 附加险
2. 调查报告
3. 保险条款
4. 公吨
5. 破碎险
6. subject to
7. with a franchise of 5%
8. Glazed Wall Tiles
9. trading company
10. Commodity Inspection Bureau

II. Fill in the blanks with the following words or expressions.

| broader coverage | take out | for buyer's account | premium | invoice value |
| according to | comply with | franchise | damage | additional risk |

1. The cover is subject to a _____ of 5%.
2. If you want _____, we shall insure this article on your own account.

CHAPTER XI   INSURANCE

3. Regarding insurance, the coverage is for 110% of the _____ up to the port of destination only.

4. Should any _____ occur, you may file a claim within 30 days after the arrival of the consignment.

5. _____ to our usual practice, we insure goods for the invoice value plus 10%.

6. The extra _____ should be borne by you.

7. We regret that we cannot _____ your request for covering insurance for 150% of the invoice value.

8. If _____ should be covered, the extra premium is for buyer's account.

9. Buyer's request for insurance to be arranged up to the inland city can be accepted on condition that such extra premium is _____.

10. We shall _____ the insurance on the goods against Breakage.

III. Translate the following sentences into English.
1. 感谢你方已按我们的特别要求投保附加险。兹附上支票一张，金额为 500 英镑，以偿还你们的保险差价。
2. 请你方立即告诉我们对你方该货物要投保的详细险别。
3. 如能告知有关中国人保财险办理的保险范围供我方参考，我们将不胜感激。
4. 如果要投附加险，额外保险费由买方负担。
5. 为了安全起见，我们建议你方为这批货物投保一切险和战争险。
6. 由于上述货物保险享有 5% 免赔率，因此本保险公司只能受理对该货物损失超过 5% 部分的索赔。

Lesson 30

Asking the Seller to Cover Insurance

　　进出口货物运输险按货物不同的运输方式主要分为海上、陆上、航空和邮包四类。中国保险条款的保险险别一般分主险（基本险）、一般附加险和特别附加险。

From: Mike@genway.com
To: Jane@jenney.com
Subject: our order No. 626 for 300 cases canned beef

Jane,

We would like you to refer to our Order No. 626 for 300 cases Canned Beef from which you will see that this order was placed on CFR basis.

As now we wish to have the captioned goods insured in your place, we shall appreciate it if you arrange to insure the consignment on our behalf against WPA, T.P.N.D., Fresh and/or Rain Water Damage Risks and War Risk for 110% of the invoice value with the People's Insurance Company of China.

We shall of course refund the premium to you on receipt of your debit note and the covering insurance policy.

Looking forward to your early reply.

Best regards,
Mike

1. **Canned Beef** 牛肉罐头
2. **on behalf of** 代表

   on behalf of the buyers 代为买方投保

   We shall insure the captioned goods on behalf of the buyer.
   我们将代为买家投保标题项下的货物。
3. **T.P.N.D.** 也可写为 TPND，全称：Theft, Pilferage & Non-Delivery Risks 偷窃、提货不着险

   Fresh and/or Rain Water Damage Risks 淡水雨淋险
   这两种险别均属于中国保险条款中的海洋运输货物保险条款所包括的附加险。
   常见的一般附加险还有：

CHAPTER XI INSURANCE

Shortage Risk 或 Risk of Shortage 短量险
Intermixture & Contamination Risks 混杂、玷污险
Leakage Risk 或 Risk of Shortage 渗漏险
Clash & Breakage Risks 碰损、破碎险
Taint of Odor Risk 串味险
Sweating & Heating Risks 受潮受热险
Hook Damage Risk 钩损险
Rust Risk 或 Risk of Rust 锈损险
Breakage of Packing Risk 包装破裂险
We shall cover TPND on your order.
我们将对你方所订的货物投保偷窃、提货不着险。
The goods are to be insured against Hook Damage Risk. 此货需保钩损险。
常见的特殊附加险有：
War Risk 战争险
Strikes, Riots and Civil Commotions（缩写为 S.R.C.C., 也可写作 SRCC）罢工、暴动、民变险（注意：这个险别没有 risks 这个词）
We insure Biscuit against of Taint of Odor Risk. 我们对饼干投保串味险。
We have insured Bed Sheet against All Risks and War risk.
我们已经对床单投保一切险和战争险。

4. **for 110% of the invoice value** 发票金额的 110%，也可写为 for the invoice value plus 10%，或 for an amount of 10% above the invoice value。
We have covered insurance on the 500 bolts of Printed Shirting for 110% of the insurance value against All Risks and War Risk.
我们已将 500 匹的印花细布按发票金额的 110% 投保一切险和战争险。

5. **invoice value** 发票金额
It is our usual practice to insure shipments for the invoice value plus 10%.
我们的惯例是按发票金额加上 10% 投保。

6. **debit note**（缩写为 D/N）借方通知
We shall refund the premium to you on receipt of your debit note.
一俟收到你们的借方通知，我们就把保险费付还你们。
credit note 贷方票据，也叫 credit invoice，抵扣发票（客户发现收到的货物质量或数量有问题，就会要求开出抵扣发票，在以后的业务中就凭借这个抵扣少付货款。）

I. Translate the following expressions into Chinese or vice versa.

1. on behalf of
2. on receipt of
3. TPND
4. Shortage Risk
5. the captioned goods
6. 借方通知
7. 钩损险
8. 渗漏险
9. 发票金额
10. 战争险

II. Complete the following sentences in English.

1. We shall cover the insurance _____（按发票金额的 110%）.
2. We are arranging _____（相关的保险单）.
3. We shall insure the goods against _____（偷窃、提货不着险）.
4. We are glad to provide the insurance _____（代为买方投保）.
5. Please insure the goods against _____（一切险和战争险）.
6. We shall refund the premium to you _____（一俟收到你方的借记通知）.

III. Translate the following letter into English.

> 敬启者：
> 　　关于我方购货确认书 212 号项下的 3500 台"康佳"牌电视机，现通知你们，我们已由中国银行开立了保兑的、不可撤销的 678 号信用证。
> 　　请注意上述货物必须在 4 月 15 日前装运。保险须按发票金额的 130% 投保一切险。我们知道按照你方的一般惯例，你们只按发票金额另加 10% 投保，因此额外的保费由我方负担。
> 　　请按我方要求办理保险，我方等候你方的装船通知。
>
> 　　　　　　　　　　　　　　　　　　　　　　　　　　　　王杰　谨上

CHAPTER XI INSURANCE

Business Link

国际贸易货物运输保险程序

在国际货物买卖过程中，由哪一方负责办理投保，应根据买卖双方商定的价格条件来确定。例如，若按 FOB 条件和 CFR 条件成交，保险即应由买方办理；如按 CIF 条件成交，就应由卖方办理。办理货运保险的一般程序是：

1. 确定投保的金额

投保金额是诸保险费的依据，又是货物发生损失后计算赔偿的依据。按照国际惯例，投保金额应按发票上的 CIF 的预期利润计算。但是，各国市场情况不尽相同，对进出口贸易的管理办法也各有异。向中国人保财险办理进出口货物运输保险，有两种办法：一种是逐笔投保；另一种是按签订的预约保险总合同办理。

2. 填写投保单

保险单是投保人向保险人提出投保的书面申请，其主要内容包括被保险人的姓名、被保险货物的品名、标记、数量及包装、保险金额、运输工具名称、开航日期及起讫地点、投保险别、投保日期及签章等。

3. 支付保险费，取得保险单

保险费按投保险别的保险费率计算。保险费率是根据不同的险别、不同的商品、不同的运输方式、不同的目的地，并参照国际上的费率水平而制定的。它分为"一般货物费率"和"指明货物加费费率"两种。前者是一般商品的费率，后者系指特别列明的货物（如某些易碎、易损商品）在一般费率的基础上另行加收的费率。

交付保险费后，投保人即可取得保险单（insurance policy）。保险单实际上已构成保险人与被保险人之间的保险契约，是保险人与被保险人的承保证明。在发生保险范围内的损失或灭失时，投保人可凭保险单要求赔偿。

4. 提出索赔手续

当被保险的货物发生属于保险责任范围内的损失时，投保人可以向保险人提出赔偿要求。按 INCOTERMS 2000 E 组、F 组、C 组包含的 8 种价格条件成交的合同，一般应由买方办理索赔。按 INCOTERMS 2000 D 组包含的 5 种价格条件成交的合同，则视情况由买方或卖方办理索赔。

被保险货物运抵目的地后，收货人如发现整件短少或有明显残损，应立即向承运人或有关方面索取货损或货差证明，并联系保险公司指定的检验理赔代理人申请检验，提出检验报告，确定损失程度；同时向承运人或有关责任方提出索赔。属于保险责任范围内的，可填写索赔清单，连同提单副本、装箱单、保险单正本、磅码单、修理配置费凭证、第三者责任方的签证或商务记录以及向第三者责任方索赔的来往函件等，向保险公司索赔。索赔应当在保险有效期内提出并办理，否则保险公司可以不予办理。

Skill Training

Exercise I. Translate the following letter into Chinese.

> Dear Melisa,
>
> Please quote us the lowest rate for floating policy on the goods mentioned below:
>
> 500 cartons of cotton goods, valued at US$26,500, going from Pusan, Korea, to Singapore by S.S. Breeze which is to set sail from Pusan on June 4. The goods are packed in strong cartons of international standard.
>
> We'd like to cover insurance against ICC(A) & War Risk. Please send us the lowest insurance rate at the earliest. Thank you in advance.
>
> Best regards,
> Bruce

Exercise II. Make out the insurance policy according to the following L/C clauses.

1. 有关信用证条款

   1) Beneficiary: Shanghai Light Industrial Imp. & Exp. Corp.

   2) Applicant

   3) Evidencing shipment of : Sports Shoes 12,600 pairs at GBP1.2 per pair CIF London

   4) Total amount: GBP15,120

   5) Document required:

   Insurance Policy or Certificate in duplicate made out to order and endorsed in blank covering All Risks and War risks as per China Insurance Clause (CIC) 1/1/1981 of The People's Insurance Company of China.

CHAPTER XI　INSURANCE

2. 有关资料

　1) Commercial Invoice No: SD 537

　2) Packing: 100 cartons

　3) Shipment from Shanghai to London per M.V. Fenjin on Sep. 15, 2020

××××× 保　险　公　司

保　险　单　　　　　保险单号次
INSURANCE POLICY

×××××　保　险　公　司　（以　下　简　称　本　公　司）
THIS POLICY OF INSURANCE WITNESSES THAT THE ××××× INSURANCE COMPANY OF CHINA (HEREINAFTER CALLED "THE COMPANY")
根　据
AT THE REQUEST OF
(以 下 简 称 被 保 险 人) 的 要 求, 由 被 保 险 人 向 本 公 司 缴 付 约
(HEREINAFTER CALLED "THE INSURED") AND IN CONSIDERATION OF THE AGREED PREMIUM PAID TO THE COMPANY BY THE
定 的 保 险, 按 照 本 保 险 单 承 保 险 别 和 背 面 所 载 条 款 下 列
INSURED UNDERTAKES TO INSURE THE UNDERMENTIONED GOODS IN TRANSPORTATION SUBJECT TO THE CONDITIONS OF THIS POLICY
特 款 承 保 下 述 货 物 运 输 保 险, 特 立 本 保 险 单
AS PER THE CLAUSES PRINTED OVERLEAF AND OTHER SPECIAL CLAUSES ATTACHED HEREON

标　记 MARKS & NOS.	包装及数量 QUANTITY	保险货物项目 DESCRIPTION OF GOODS	保　险　金　额 AMOUNT INSURED

总 保 险 金 额:
TOTAL AMOUNT INSURED:

保　费　　　　　　费　率　　　　　　装 载 运 输 工 具
PREMIUM　　　　　RATE　　　　　　PER CONVEYANCE SS.

开　航　日　期　　　　　自　　　　　　　　　　　　　　　　　至
SLG. ON OR ABT.　　　　FROM　　　　　　　　　　　　　　　　　TO

承保险别:
CONDITIONS

所 保 货 物, 如 遇 出 险, 本 公 司 凭 本 保 险 单 及 其 他 有 关 证 件 给 付 赔 款.
CLAIMS, IF ANY, PAYABLE ON SURRENDER OF THIS POLICY TOGETHER WITH OTHER RELEVANT DOCUMENTS
所 保 货 物, 如 发 生 本 保 险 单 项 下 负 责 赔 偿 的 损 失 或 事 故,
IN THE EVENT OF ACCIDENT WHEREBY LOSS OR DAMAGE MAY RESULT IN A CLAIM UNDER THIS POLICY IMMEDIATE NOTICE
应 立 即 通 知 本 公 司 下 述 代 理 人 查 勘.
APPLYING FOR SURVEY MUST BE GIVEN TO THE COMPANY'S AGENT AS MENTIONED HEREUNDER:

××××× 保险公司上海分公司
THE ××××× INSURANCE CO. OF CHINA
SHANGHAI BRANCH

赔　款　偿　付　地　点
CLAIM PAYABLE AT/IN
日　期　　　　　　　　　上海
DATE　　　　　　　　　SHANGHAI　　　　　　　　　General Manager
地址:中国上海××路××号
Address: ×× Lu Shanghai, China.

Useful Expressions

1. For transactions concluded on CIF basis, we usually cover the insurance against All Risks for 110% of the full invoice value with the People's Insurance Company of China as per CIC of the 1st January, 1981.
2. The differences between CIF and CFR prices depends on the nature of the goods to be insured, the degree of coverage desired and the place of destination.
3. Your request for insurance to be covered for 150% of the invoice value can be met but the premium for the difference between 150% and 110% should be for your account.
4. We adopt the warehouse to warehouse clause which is commonly used in international insurance.
5. We cannot comply with your request for insuring your order for 130% of its invoice value.
6. This kind of additional risk is coverable at 2‰. This risk is coverable at a premium of 0.35%.
7. Insurance on the goods shall be covered by us for 110% of the CIF value, and any extra premium for additional coverage, if required, shall be borne by the buyers.
8. The cover shall be limited to sixty days upon discharge of the insured goods from the seagoing vessel at the final port of discharge.
9. Our underwriter has surveyors and agents in practically all the big cities in the world to handle claims. Should any damage occur to the goods a claim may be filed with the insurance agent at your end with the necessary documents.
10. If you have an open policy with your insurance company we do not object to your covering insurance at your end and in that case we will advise you of the particulars of the shipment as soon as we ship the goods.
11. Please quote your lowest rate for floating policy of $10,000 against WPA, general merchandise, in wooden cases only per S.S. Queen from Shanghai to Liverpool.
12. We have noted that you require the insurance to be covered against Risk of Breakage. However, please be informed that our CIF prices include insurance to cover WPA only and if you wish to have the Risk of Breakage included in the coverage, you must bear the additional premium.

CHAPTER XI INSURANCE

13. The insured should promptly submit an insurance claim to the insurer or its agent so as to provide the latter with ample time to pursue recovery from the relative party in fault.
14. The premium rates quoted to us do not meet our expectations. Therefore, we are unable to sign a general policy with your company at this time.
15. You're required to submit the following documents in presenting a claim to our agent: Original Policy or Certificate of Insurance, original or copy of B/L, Invoice and Packing List, Certificate of Loss or Damage, Survey Report and Statement of Claim.

CHAPTER XII
COMPLAINTS, CLAIMS AND SETTLEMENT

Objectives:
After learning this chapter, you will
1. grasp basic terms related to complaints and claims.
2. learn the way of writing complaints and claims.
3. be familiar with the style of the complaint and claim letters.
4. identify the approach of writing complaint and claim letters.

Introduction

买卖合同一经订立，缔约双方必须严格遵守合同的规定，履行各自的义务。但是在实际业务中，由于各种原因，不履行或不完全按照合同规定履行合同的情况是经常发生的。在这种情况下，往往产生争议，引起索赔和理赔的问题。所谓索赔（claim），是指遭受损害的一方在争议发生后，根据合同或法律的有关规定，向违约方（defaulting party）提出赔偿（indemnity）要求。所谓理赔（settlement），是指违约方对遭受损失的一方所提出的赔偿要求的受理。

索赔和理赔必须经过调查研究，实事求是地处理。在我国进出口业务中，履行出口合同时，多系外商向我方索赔；履行进口合同时，则由我方向外商索赔的情况较多。

索赔必须在合同规定的有效期内提出（一般规定是在货到后三十天内提出），若超过有效期则无权向对方提出索赔。在国际贸易中，通常采用协商方法来解决争议。如双方协商后仍得不到解决，则一般可采取调解（reconciliation）和仲裁（arbitration）的方式，个别情况下才通过诉讼（lawsuit）方式来处理。

在本章中，我们主要介绍货物因包装以及质量问题而引起的申诉、索赔和理赔。

CHAPTER XII COMPLAINTS, CLAIMS AND SETTLEMENT

Writing Strategy

书写索赔信通常遵循下列步骤：
1. 信的开头应对提出的抱怨或索赔表示遗憾。
2. 说明订单日期、交货日期及所索赔的货物。
3. 说明不满的原因。
4. 提及由此而引起的不便，并要求予以解释。
5. 提出如何纠正的建议。

收到索赔信时，要尽快妥善、合理地解决问题，尽量避免诉讼和仲裁。具体的写作步骤如下：
1. 提及信件。
2. 对已发生的损失应表示歉意或遗憾。
3. 礼貌地就对方提出的意见和解决方法作出回复，提出意见和补救措施。
4. 良好愿望的表达。

Lesson 31

Claim on Export Carton

包装包括很多细节，如内包装、标贴、条形码和唛头等，一不注意就会引起错误。由于业务员疏忽大意，造成外箱唛头错误，买方大为恼火。本篇邮件语气直接，有大量单词大写，可以看出买方的情绪，所以业务员操作时，一定要谨慎，跟买方确认细节。还好是长久合作的关系，买方没有取消订单，但此类事情绝不可以再次产生，因为竞争是非常激烈的。

From: Lisa@genway.com.es
To: Celia@tchina.com
Date: 5 December, 2018 11: 49
Subject: export carton

Celia,

There are a lot of problems with the EXPORT CARTONS:

On the orders of VELCRO there is written FASCIA on the cartons!!

On orders of PROTTI 333 TO 337 there is not written PROTTI.

On order of LUNGA 328, 329, 340, 341 there is not written LUNGA.

WHEN I SEND YOU ORDERS WITH SHIPPING MARKS YOU HAVE TO COPY EXACTLY AS I WRITE TO YOU!!

NOW ALL THE CLIENTS THAT WILL RECEIVE THESE VELCRO WILL CALL TO TELL US THAT IS WRONG AND THIS IS VERY ANNOYING!

For next shipments, make sure there is written Velcro on the export cartons otherwise I will not release you the inspection certificate.

Lisa

1. **claim** *n./v.* 索赔

    make/file/lodge/register/raise/put in/bring up a claim (against sb.) /(for/on sth.) 向……提出索赔

    They submitted a claim on this shipment for $5,000 on account of short weight.
    由于这批货重量不足，我们索赔 5000 美元。

    On the basis of survey report, we lodge our claim with/against/on you for US$10,000.
    依据调查报告，我们向你索赔 10,000 美元。

    accept/admit a claim 同意索赔   entertain a claim 受理索赔

CHAPTER XII COMPLAINTS, CLAIMS AND SETTLEMENT

dismiss a claim 驳回索赔 withdraw a claim 索赔
reject a claim 拒绝索赔 waive a claim 放弃索赔

2. **velcro** *n.* 尼龙搭扣，魔术贴
3. **PROTTI** 意大利电脑横机品牌，电脑横机是一种双针板舌针纬编织织机。
4. **make sure** 确信，证实
   Make sure you've signed the cheque before sealing the envelope.
   一定要在支票上签了名再封信封。
5. **release** *vt./n.* 释放；发布；让与
   This payment will release you from any further obligation to the company.
   付了这笔钱之后，你对公司就再也没有别的债务了。
   Prices blipped a shade higher still following the release of GNP figures.
   国民生产总值的数字公布后价格又上涨了一点。
6. **inspection certificate** 检验证明书，检查证明
   Enclosed is a copy of the inspection certificate from our quality control department.
   随函附上本公司质量监控部门出具的一份检验证书。
   Our Inspection Bureau will issue a Veterinary Inspection Certificate to show that the shipment is in conformity with export standards.
   商检局将出具动物检疫证明书以证明货物符合出口标准。

I. Translate the following expressions into Chinese or vice versa.

1. authentic surveyor
2. inspection certificate
3. export carton
4. waive a claim
5. make sure
6. 提出索赔
7. 同意索赔
8. 拒绝索赔
9. 撤回索赔
10. 唛头

II. Fill in the blanks with the following words or expressions.

| took delivery of | lodge a complaint | replacement | faulty | supplied to |
| have no choice but to | dispatch | are prepared to | agree to | resulted from |

1. Since you have delayed the shipment, we _____ cancel the contract.
2. It is obvious that the damage to the goods _____ the rough handling.
3. Your cooperation in this instance is very much appreciated and we trust the _____ will reach you in due course.
4. If your business with us turns out to our satisfaction, we will _____ renew the Agency Agreement.
5. The _____ quality of the goods received will no doubt affect the selling price.
6. On arrival of M.V. "Castle" at Port Louis, we _____ the consignment.
7. We _____ repack the goods at the warehouse.
8. The carpets _____ our Order No. C396 of July 3 have arrived this morning.
9. Your last shipment is so disappointing that I have to _____ against you.
10. Please _____ the replacement according to our order.

III. Letter-writing practice.

Write a letter in proper form according to the following situation.

Suppose you are an American buyer (American DDD Trading Co., Ltd.) who has ordered 500 tins of green tea from China Zhenyuan Trade Co., Ltd. Upon arrival at New York port, 50 tins were found completely wet. You write a letter lodging a claim against this.

Commodity:	Longjing Green Tea
Price:	CNY38/tin FOB New York
Quantity:	1,200 tins
Packing:	Export Standard
Specification:	First Class
Address of Buyer:	P.O. Box 58090 Santa Clara California USA 95052-8090
Address of Seller:	No. 13 Zhen An Road Guangzhou Guangdong China

CHAPTER XII COMPLAINTS, CLAIMS AND SETTLEMENT

Lesson 32

Settling Complaint

买方与卖方之间往往还有中间商，中间商要协调好双方的矛盾，摆出事实，算出成本，再决定方案，对双方理解都比较容易。

From: farah @sales.zzqx.com.cn
To: steve_guan@Skyfood.com
Subject: order No. 08-1103-23

Dear Ravin,

There are three issues which I would like to bring to your attention and resolve with your input:

1) MC089

We paid USD4497.60 on 14th June, not USD2,000.

2) barcode issue

Now it seems that they complained me why I didn't print it myself?
The problem was that some barcodes are missing, and shouldn't I ask them to re-print?

3) L95 reject 4,000 pairs

Regarding the issue of the 4,000 rejected pairs. Prior to taking a decision, I want to bring to your notice the costs and expenses already incurred on these goods:

Pairs	: 4,000
Per Pair Cost	: USD1.32
Cost of Goods	: USD5,280.00
Handling Charges @ 6%	: USD316.80
China Local Expenses Appx. 3.31%	: USD174.77
(A) Total Cost in USD	: USD5771.57
Custom Duty Paid	: Rs107,384.00
Local Clearing & Transportation Charges	: Rs52,000.00
Total Indian Expenses	: Rs159,384.00
(B) In USD @ 83.16	: USD1916.59
Total (A)+(B)	: USD7688.16

If we go ahead and remake the shoes, we will again incur the clearing cost and the local expenses of the shoes. Because these are for our budget brand, they were priced very aggressively. According to me, returning the pairs to China and remaking them and getting them back does not make any sense. Furthermore, I cannot understand how so many pairs came through without the normal quality check which you are so strict about.

Pls advise on how we should go ahead on the above three matters.

Thanks & regards,
Farah

1. **complain** *vi.* 投诉，抱怨

    complain about sth. 投诉某事

    We have to complain about the inferior quality of the ball-pens.

    我们要投诉圆珠笔的不良品质。

    The buyer complained to the seller of the late delivery.

    买方向卖方抱怨货物延误。

2. **bring to your attention** 提请你方注意……

    类似的还有：draw/call/invite/direct your attention to...

    However we must persevere and bring to your attention some critical issues regarding names that contain special characters.

    但是我们必须让您注意一些有关名称中包含特殊字符的严重问题。

    We wish to draw your attention to the expiration date of the L/C.

    我方想提请你方注意信用证的到期日。

    We wish to call your attention to the fact that as the goods are very easily damaged by heat, we hope that you will keep them in a cool place.

    我们提请你方注意货物受热易坏的现象，希望你方能把货物储藏在阴凉之地。

3. **resolve** *vi.* 解决

    The government is deliberating about what should be done to resolve the problem.

    政府对采取什么措施来解决这个问题进行了慎重考虑。

CHAPTER XII   COMPLAINTS, CLAIMS AND SETTLEMENT

4. rejected *adj.* 被拒的；不合格的

His application was rejected out of hand. 他的申请立即遭到拒绝。

5. incur *v.* 招致；遭受

Any out-of-pocket expenses incurred on the firm's business will be reimbursed.

因公司业务产生的开销都可以报销。

6. handling charges 手续费

Figure 2 shows a decision table that assigns shipping and handling charges for various combinations of package weight and volume.

图 2 显示了为包裹的各种重量与体积组合分配运输和处理费用的决策表。

I. Translate the following expressions into Chinese or vice versa.

1. settling complaint
2. custom duty paid
3. budget brand
4. prior to
5. normal quality
6. 货物成本
7. 解决问题
8. 手续费
9. 商检局
10. 提请你方注意

II. Fill in the blanks with proper prepositions.

1. The buyers are complaining _____ the wrong goods _____ the sellers.
2. We are holding the goods of faulty goods _____ your disposal.
3. As the damage occurred during transit, please direct your claim _____ the insurance company.
4. Our clients have claimed _____ us _____ delayed delivery of the goods.
5. We regret to say that we have to lodge our claim _____ the Arbitration Committee.
6. This delay is causing us serious inconvenience because we promises delivery _____ the strength of your assurance.
7. The shipment is short-invoiced _____ RMB ¥8,600 and we have drawn a draft on you _____ the balance.
8. Please fax your confirmation on receipt of our remittance for US$5,000 in settlement _____ the claim.

9. We wish to call your attention _____ the fact that as the goods are very easily damaged _____ heat.

III. Translate the following letter into English.

> 敬启者：
>
>   关于贵方 10,000 个机器零件的索赔
>
>   继我方 5 月 16 日传真，兹通知贵方我方代表已对此事进行了调查，发现是我方货仓职员的工作失误，所以，我方将进行理赔。
>
>   但是我方建议的解决方式是我方立即发运质量保证的替代物。至于贵方收到我方的机器零件，如果能代我方在贵方市场销售，我方将不胜感激。售价按我方报价，即每个 18 美元，包括你方 3% 的佣金。若贵方同意上述意见，请以传真告知我方。
>
>   此事给贵方带来了麻烦，在此深表歉意，并向贵方保证我方将采取一切措施避免此类差错再次发生。
>
> 谨上

Lesson 33

Settlement on Inferior Quality

  出货是外贸业务中最后一个环节。延期交货在某些行业里也是司空见惯的事情，或者是在出货过程中，由于货物太多搬运损坏货物或者发错货，因此引发的一系列问题也是让人头痛不已。外贸人员要锻炼应对这些难题的能力，争取将损失降到最低。本案例是货物在出厂前检验发现问题，这时无法赶货，于是采取了几套方案解决。用近似鞋款替代先前的货物，赔偿被损坏的鞋子，并征询客户的意见。

> From: Winnie@hotmail.com
> To: Josef @public.xm.fj.cn
> Subject: short or mix shipment for Szech order
>
> Hi Josef/Vladimir,
>
> Re: short or mix shipment for Szech order

CHAPTER XII COMPLAINTS, CLAIMS AND SETTLEMENT

The goods were shipped out on time.

10 pairs of outsoles were defect & damaged during mass production. The outsole factory could not replace before our delivery. We did not want to ship inferior quality shoes, so we replaced other nearest sizes (same styles) for short delivery: total 4 cartons (with slightly different sizes). We suggest returning the amount for below 5 pairs short shipment by cash refund during your visit on 8/29. Please review & comment.

ARTICLE	CTN#	EU SIZE PAIRS	ACTUAL PAIRS			REMARKS
H0 263 201	1325#	43# 10	43# 8			2 PAIRS WERE SHORT DELIVERY
TR 050 327	585#	40# 10	40# 8	31# 1	38# 1	USE 31# and 38# FOR REPLACEMENT
TR 058 327	1094#	39# 10	39# 8	31# 1	38# 1	USE 31# and 38# FOR REPLACEMENT
TR 054 327	726#	38# 10	38# 7			3 PAIRS WERE SHORT DELIVERY

We apologize for the inconveniences caused to you.

Best regards,
Winnie

1. **short** *adj.* 短的，不足的，矮的，低的
    short-weight 重量不足，短重
    short delivery 短交，缺交
    short shipment 短装，装载不足
    short-calculated 少算的
    short-delivered 短交的，缺交的
    short-landed 短卸的
    short-shipped 短装的

short-paid 少付的

short unloaded 短卸的

2. **defect** *n.* 缺点，缺陷，不足之处

About 20 percent of the defects cause 80 percent of all errors.

大约 20% 的缺陷所造成的错误占所有错误的 80%。

3. **mass production** 批量生产；规模生产

That kind of scale is why some executives believe that China could be the country in which electric vehicles move from the concept stage to mass production.

由于规模如此大，一些汽车业主管认为中国可能成为使电动汽车由概念转向大规模生产得以实现的国家。

4. **replace** *vt.* 取代，替换，更换

However, this will replace all of your work in this project, so backup anything you want to keep.

不过，这将替换您在此项目中的所有工作，所以，请备份您需要保存的任何内容。

replacement *n.* 顶替，更换

Replacement is guaranteed if the products are not up to the standard.

产品不合规格，保证退换。

5. **cash refund** 现金退还，退税柜台

If you have the receipt, I can give you a cash refund.

你有发票的话，我可以把现金退还给你。

6. **review** *v.* 复查，复审，复核

Salaries are kept under constant review. 薪金问题要一直不断审订。

I. Translate the following expressions into Chinese or vice versa.

1. short delivery
2. short-weight
3. short unloaded
4. replacement
5. surveyor's report

6. 劣质
7. 引起麻烦
8. 少算
9. 现金退还
10. 索赔清单

CHAPTER XII　COMPLAINTS, CLAIMS AND SETTLEMENT

II. Translate the following sentences into English.

1. 出入镜检验检疫局对第 A105 号订单下货物因质量低劣提出的索赔进行了详细调查。
2. 因为短重我们要向你方就这批货提出索赔，金额为 3200 美元。
3. 我们很惊奇地发现货物的质量低于样品的质量。
4. 请告知受损货物是交由我方处理，还是退还现金。
5. 买方对卖方迟交货提出投诉。

III. Translate the following letter into English.

敬启者：

　　有关上周发运的第 343 号订单的来信收悉。

　　对于货物在运送途中破损的事宜，本公司感到遗憾。本公司一向特别小心包装货物，然而不当的运输方法亦会引起损坏。

　　本公司将按照贵公司开列的破损货物清单更换新货，不日将运抵贵处。

　　已就有关损失向保险公司索偿，烦请保留破损货物供保险公司检查。

　　不便之处，敬请见谅。

谨上

Business Link

complaint 申诉方
defendant 被诉方
appeal（解决争端）上诉
short delivery 短交
short unloaded 短卸的
lost in transit 短失，在运输过程中丢失
survey report 公证报告
damage report 破损证书
marine protest 海难报告
claim assessor 估损人
claim settling agent 理赔代理人
claim survey agent 理赔检验代理人
claim letter 索赔书

claim document 索赔证件
claim settlement 理赔
claim indemnity 索赔
claim department 索赔委员会

Skill Training

Exercise I. Draft a letter to the company, complaining about wrong dispatch as mentioned below.

Background: Some time ago you placed this order with CMA Advertising Gifts.

Order No: 03443
Pocket Radios

Quantity	Description	Price	Total
50	W1/787 Pocket Radios	$26.95	$1347.50

The delivery arrived this morning. When you unpacked the goods you found 50 pocket calculators.

Write an email to CMA Advertising Gifts complaining about wrong dispatch.

Exercise II. You have just received the complaint below. Decide upon an action that will correct the situation and write an adjustment letter to satisfy the customer.

Re: Claim for Our Loss

Dear Tom,

We have received your shipment of 500 electric calculators on our Order No. 453-90.

While appreciating your prompt shipment, we are surprised to find two cases labeled as C/No. 20 and 450 were broken with the result that 40 electric calculators contained

CHAPTER XII COMPLAINTS, CLAIMS AND SETTLEMENT

were damaged to various degrees. We think the packing is not strong enough to protect the goods and the wooden materials should have been thicker.

We informed an authorized surveyor at once, who examined the goods in the presence of the shipping company's agents, and we are sure the enclosed surveyor's report will prove our view to be right.

Under such circumstances, we shall have to dispose of the damaged cameras at a greatly reduced price below 50% of their invoice cost. Therefore, we suggest you make us an allowance to make up for the loss according, say, $50 for each damaged camera.

Looking forward to your comments.

Best regards,
Leo

Useful Expressions

1. I am writing for a replacement of the dictionary included.
2. Would you please correct your shipment by sending the order No. by the first available vessel?
3. It would be highly appreciated if you could look into the personal computers, which should have reached our destination two weeks ago.
4. We feel it necessary to inform you that your last delivery of our order is not up to the usual standard.
5. Upon inspection, it was found that the total content had been short-delivered by...tons.
6. On comparing the goods received with the sample supplied, we were sorry to notice the great differences in the designs of the machines.
7. After having the boxes examined we found that they were not strong enough for long distance delivery.
8. It is regrettable to see that the chemical content of Item is not up to the percentage contracted.

9. There is a discrepancy in colors between the received materials and the samples.
10. While placing our order we emphasized that any delay in delivery would definitely add to the cost of the goods. That is why we have to raise a claim on refunds for the loss incurred.
11. The inspection report shows a report weight of 12 tons. And upon analysis, excessive moisture was found and that accounted for another 12 tons.
12. Your claim for shortage of weight amounts to USD1,000 in all.
13. We regret to learn that 3 cases out of the 10 shipped against your Order No.100 arrived in a badly damaged condition. As the goods were packed with the greatest care, we can only presume that the cases have been roughly handled.
14. We thank you for sending us the sample of inferior goods for examination and we have passed it onto the manufacturers for inspection. Evidently, through an oversight some of the wrong goods were dispatched to you.
15. I'm afraid I have to insist that you approach the insurance company for the settlement, that is, if you have included this risk in your coverage.

APPENDIX

TEST
外销员考试模拟题

I. Translation of terms. (10 Points)

A. Translate the following terms into Chinese. (5 Points)

1. FCA
2. TRIMs
3. T.P.N.D.
4. Composite index
5. G.A.
6. Voyage charter
7. Endorsement
8. Straight bill of lading
9. Rebate
10. Auction

B. Translate the following terms into English in full. (5 Points)

1. 议付
2. 保函
3. （代理业务中的）委托人
4. 无追索权
5. 市场准入
6. 电子商务认证
7. 领事发票
8. 循环信用证
9. 贸易壁垒
10. 北美自由贸易协定

II. Make the best choice for each of the following sentence. (25 points)

1. Owing to the unforeseen difficulties, the factory cannot send the goods to us _____ schedule.
   A. before   B. behind   C. in   D. on

2. We shall inform you _____ the date of shipment.
   A. at   B. in   C. of   D. to

3. The boxes are likely to receive rough handing at this end and must be able to withstand transport _____ very bad roads.
   A. against   B. for   C. in   D. over

4. The goods under our order No. 020531C were received yesterday, and we have now examined them _____ your enclosed lists and invoices.
   A. against   B. before   C. on   D. with

5. Your price is too high to interest our buyers _____ a counter offer.
   A. making   B. in making   C. make   D. to be made

6. Enclosed are two copies of our Sales Confirmation No. DTE02064 _____ out against your Order KK02736.
   A. blow   B. made   C. let   D. taking

7. Some customers requested us to _____ our price because they consider it too high.
   A. bring down   B. get down   C. put down   D. take down

8. Our corporation _____ foodstuffs.
   A. deals   B. handles   C. handles in   D. specializes

9. Please _____ us for the supply of the items in the enclosed in inquiry from.
   A. give   B. offer   C. quote   D. send

10. We would be prepared to review this once we have established a firm _____ association with you.
    A. trade   B. traded   C. trading   D. trades

11. We can allow you a special discount of 12% on orders exceeding $60,000. The word "allow" can be replaced by the following words EXCEPT _____
    A. give   B. grant   C. offer   D. permit

12. We have arranged with the Bank of Japan, Tokyo, to _____ a credit in your favor to be available until September 30.
    A. draw   B. establish   C. make   D. quote

13. We have received the document and _____ delivery of the above order which arrived at our port on the M.V. Toho Maru.
    A. collected   B. effected   C. made   D. taken

APPENDIX

14. We have pleased to enclose a _____ quotation for bathroom showers.
    A. detail   B. detailed   C. detailing   D. details
15. The consignment was shipped _____ on the S.S. Changfeng which left Shanghai for Singapore on June 16.
    A. clean   B. cleaned   C. cleaning   D. cleanly
16. Mr. Wang _____ charge of our sales in Europe.
    All of the following can be used here EXCEPT _____.
    A. has been put in B. has taken   C. is in   D. is in the
17. For your own _____ please expedite the L/C, which must reach us before August 7.
    A. advantage   B. benefit   C. consideration   D. profit
18. In the _____ we should ask you to dispatch the replacement to us as soon as possible.
    A. meantime   B. meanwhile   C. time   D. occasion
19. This will enable us to arrange speedy passage through Customs on _____ of the consignment.
    A. arrival   B. arriving   C. reception   D. receiving
20. The supply is inadequate to meet the _____.
    A. demand   B. purchase   C. conquest   D. require
21. Our policy with regard to contractual agreement does not allow _____ of legal rights.
    A. waive   B. waiver   C. wave   D. waver
22. If any information that you send us is confidential, it shall be retained _____.
    A. as such   B. at such   C. such as   D. such that
23. Our illustrated catalog _____ shows various types of bathroom fittings and the sizes available.
    A. also enclosed   B. that also enclosed
    C. is also enclosed   D. whish also enclosed
24. A container holds 240 bicycles; the whole cargo would therefore comprise 50 containers, _____ 8 tons.
    A. and each weighting   B. each to weight
    C. each weighting   D. each weights
25. The case should be _____ they can easily be made fast again after being opened.
    A. as such so as   B. like this so that
    C. of such a type that   D. of such a type which

227

III. Translate the following letter into English in a proper format. (20 Points)

Sanders Durables Pry, Ltd.
34 Queensland Road
Melbourne, 3400, Australia

先生/女士：

很高兴收到你方7月8日来函，询问我公司能否提供3000套家用空调机（货号：TW0203）。很遗憾地告知你方，所提商品暂时无货。

为满足你公司需求，现推荐一种新款变频（Adjustable-speed）空调。在质量上它与你所询问的分体机（split-type）一样好，但性能更加稳定，能耗降低高达15%且价格要低20%。这种空调已在中国非常畅销，相信也会在贵国市场受到欢迎。

随函寄上我司出口价格和详细的交易条件。期盼收到你们的订单。

谨上

中国北京四方电器公司
出口部经理　张建国
2022年7月14日

IV. Fill in the contract in English with information gathered from the following emails. (20 points)

Email 1

Sender: Cathy Jones <cathy@hotmail.com>
Receiver: Wang Feng<wangf@yahoo.com>
Subject: teapots
Date: 22-05-15 15: 58: 00

Shandong Eastern General Trading Co., Shandong, China

Dear Mr. Wang,

How are you?

I'm glad to tell you that our customers are very satisfied with your last shipment of brown ceramic teapots delivered to us two months ago. They have placed a new order for your teapots as follow:

　　　　Item # TP5203E/J2 (2-cup capacity)　　　480 PCS, 48 PCS/CTN
　　　　Item # TP5205E/J2 (6-cup capacity)　　　1680 PCS, 24 PCS/CTN
　　　　Item # TP5208E/J2 (10-cup capacity)　　　1206 PCS, 18 PCS/CTN

Do the prices remain the same? Could you advise your earliest date of delivery when confirming the order?

Thanks and best regards,

Unitrade Co., Ltd./Cathy Jones

Email 2

Sender: Wang Feng<wangf@yahoo.com>
Receiver: Cathy Jones <cathy@hotmail.com>
Subject: teapots
Date: 22-05-16 09: 53: 00

Unitrade Co., Ltd.

Dear Miss Jones,

Thank you for your new order. I'm glad to say we can supply the teapots you require on the usual terms. Our price remain unchanged, i.e.,

Ceramic Teapots, Brown	FOB Qingdao
Item # TP5203E/J2 (2-cup capacity)	USD@6.20/dz
Item # TP5205E/J2 (6-cup capacity)	USD@10.16/dz
Item # TP5208E/J2 (10-cup capacity)	USD@22.06/dz

We can deliver them in July.

If the above is acceptable, please confirm.

Thanks for your kind cooperation!

B. rgds,

Wang Feng

For Shandong Eastern General Trading Co., Shandong, China

Email 3

Sender: Cathy Jones <cathy@hotmail.com>
Receiver: Wang Feng<wangf@yahoo.com>
Subject: teapots
Attachment: Purchase Order
Date: 22-05-17 14: 14: 00

Dear Mr. Wang,

The price are quire acceptable. Attached I our Purchase Order No. 7033.

If there is any question, please don't hesitate to ask me.

Thanks and best regards,

Unitrade Co., Ltd./Cathy Jones

Attachment:

PURCHASE ORDER NO. 7033

To: Messrs. Shandong Eastern General Trading Co.

Commodity: Brown Ceramic Teapots

Specifications, quantity and price as stated in your email of May 16.

Finish: brown color

Packing: each piece in a cardboard box marked with UCP bar code and importer's address

Loading: in a 20ft container

Shipment: from Qingdao to Toronto on or before July 30, 2022

Shipping company: Panalpina

Shipping marks:

 D.J.C.L

TORONTO, CANADA

Item # TP5203E/J2

Item # TP5205E/J2

Item # TP5208E/J2

C/NO. 1-UP

Payment: by T/T

Inspection: before shipment

Please mention the following statement on the B/L: "We hereby certify that this shipment contains no solid-wood packing material."

Please arrange 2 PCS shipment sample of each item.

Special requirements:

GSP China from A in duplicate

Consignee and notify party for GSE from A and B/L:

Don Joy Canada Limited

281 Frosherbi Drive

Warterboo, Ontario

N2V 2G4 Canada

Unitrade Co., Ltd.

Authorized Signature(s)

Email 4

Sender: Wang Feng<wangf@yahoo.com>

Receiver: Cathy Jones <cathy@hotmail.com>

Subject: teapots

Date: 22-05-18 11: 33: 00

Dear Miss Jones,

Your email of May 17 and P/O No. 7033 have been received. Thanks.

Everything is fine, but after recalculation, we find the quantity you order adds up to only 20CBM, which is not enough to make an FCL TUE. In order to make full use of the shipping container and save shipping cost, would you please consider increasing the quantity as follows:

        Item # TP5203E/J2   1296 PCS

        Item # TP5205E/J2   2280 PCS

        Item # TP5208E/J2   1638 PCS

The above quantity fills a 20-foot container.

Please check and advise us if this workable.

With best regards,

Wang Feng

Email 5

Sander: Cathy Jones <cathy@hotmail.com>

Receiver: Wang Feng<wangf@yahoo.com>

Subject: teapots

Date: 22-05-19 09: 25: 00

Dear Mr. Wang,

How are you!

I've discussed with my buyers the possibility of increasing the quantity. Because they have already confirmed the order in the original quantity (as attached in my email dated May 17), they find it a little difficult to increase your proposal. But they say they will consider it if you may re-quote your best price!

Thanks and waiting your early reply!

Unitrade Co., Ltd./Cathy Jones

Email 6

Sender: Wang Feng<wangf@yahoo.com>

Receiver: Cathy Jones <cathy@hotmail.com>

Subject: teapots

Date: 22-05-19 16: 53: 00

Dear Miss Jones,

I've studied your proposal with my manager and am glad to inform you that we have revised the prices as follows:

  Ceramic Teapots, Brown   FOB Qingdao
  Item # TP5203E/J2 (2-cup capacity) USD@6.06/dz
  Item # TP5205E/J2 (6-cup capacity) USD@10.02/dz
  Item # TP5208E/J2 (10-cup capacity) USD@21.92/dz

Other terms remain unchanged.

Please advise whether the above is acceptable.

Awaiting your early reply!

Wang Feng
For Shandong Eastern General Trading Co.

Email 7

Sender: Cathy Jones <cathy@hotmail.com>

Receiver: Wang Feng<wangf@yahoo.com>

Subject: teapots
Date: 22-05-20 14: 29: 00

Dear Mr. Wang,

Please be informed that our Canadian buyer has agreed to increase the quantity at the revised prices to fill a 20ft container, but the quantity will be as below:

        Item # TP5203E/J2   1296 PCS, 48 PCS/CTN
        Item # TP5205E/J2   2616 PCS, 24 PCS/CTN
        Item # TP5208E/J2   1206 PCS, 18 PCS/CTN

We will send you a revised P/O later.

Please just proceed with the order if it suit you.

B. rgds,
Unitrade Co., Ltd./Cathy Jones

Email 8

Sender: Wang Feng<wangf@yahoo.com>
Receiver: Cathy Jones <cathy@hotmail.com>
Subject: teapots
Date: 22-05-21 08: 09: 00

Dear Miss Jones,

The quantity you propose is all right.
Please send your revised Purchase Order ASAP. Meanwhile, we will also send you a sales contract.

Thank you for your kind cooperation and we hope we can receive more orders from you.

Best regards,
Wang Feng
For Shandong Eastern General Trading Co.

CONTRACT No. ST2002-5-C

Sellers:
Buyers:

This contract is made by and between the buyers and the sellers, whereby the buyers agree to buy and the sellers agree to sell the under mentioned according to the terms and conditions stipulated below:

Specifications	Quantity	Unit Price	Total Value
Total amount			

Packing:

Shipping Marks:

Insurance:

Time of Shipment:

Port of Shipment:

Port of Destination:

Terms of Payment:

Done and signed in Qingdao on this 22nd day of May, 2002.

V. Write a letter in English asking for amendments to the following letter of credit by checking it with the terms of the given contract. （15 Points）

Deutsche Bank AG

Date: April 9, 2022

To Bank of China, Guangzhou

We hereby open our Irrevocable Letter of Credit No. 6785 in favor of Guangzhou Textiles Corporation for account of Schmitz & GmBH, Hamburg, Germany up to an aggregate amount of EUR24,000 (Say twenty-four thousand Euros Only) CIFC2% Hamburg for 100% of the invoice value relative to the shipment of:

6,000 yards of Pongee silk Art. No. 6103 at EUR4.80 per yard as per Contract No. 1122 dated February 15, 2022 from Guangzhou, China to Hamburg, Germany.

Drafts to be drawn at sight on our bank and accompanied by the following documents:

—Signed Commercial Invoice in triplicate;

—Full set of clean on board bills of lading made out to our order quoting L/C

No. 6785 marked "Freight Collect";

—One original marine insurance policy or certificate for 130% of the invoice value covering All Risks and War Risks, with claims payable in Germany in the currency of draft(s).

Partial shipments and transshipment are prohibited.

Shipment must be effected not later than May 31, 2022.

Draft(s) drawn under this credit must be negotiated in Germany on or before June 5, 2022.

1122 号合同主要条款：
卖方：广州纺织品公司
买方：史密茨有限公司，德国汉堡
商品名称：府绸
规格：6103 号
数量：6000 码
单价：CIF 汉堡每码 4.80 欧元，含佣金 2%
总值：28,800 欧元
装运期：2022 年 5 月由中国广州运往德国汉堡，允许分批装运和转船
保险：由卖方按发票金额的 110% 投保一切险和战争险
付款：按货物金额 100% 开立以卖方为受益人的不可撤销的即期信用证，凭卖方汇票议付

VI. Translation of passages. (10 Points)

A. From English into Chinese (5 points)

Before obtaining a large order, an exporter must check that he has the necessary cash to finance the contract—he may not receive payment for the goods until some time in the future. In certain circumstances he may be able to ask for payment in advance of the order. However, in most cases he will have to product the goods and deliver them to the market before been paid. Terms of payment are therefore important. An exporter must state the payment terms clearly and definitely and make sure that there will be no misunderstanding between exporter and importer, especially when the transaction involves a large amount of money.

B. From Chinese into English (5 points)

我们必须优化传统的出口商品结构，靠价格和数量竞争的时代已经一去不复返了。在当今竞争激烈的国际市场上，只有以质取胜和改善售前、售后服务才能行得通。

要通过精加工和深加工提高出口商品的附加值,要努力生产适销对路的名优特新产品和"拳头产品"打入国际市场。由于市场形势千变万化,出口产品必须不断地更新换代,做到你无我有、你有我优、胜人一筹。